符号中国 SIGNS OF CHINA

中国传统游戏

CHINESE TRADITIONAL GAMES

"符号中国"编写组 ◎ 编著

中央民族大学出版社
China Minzu University Press

图书在版编目(CIP)数据

中国传统游戏：汉文、英文 /"符号中国"编写组编著. —北京：中央民族大学出版社，2024.9
（符号中国）
ISBN 978-7-5660-2334-6

Ⅰ.①中… Ⅱ.①符… Ⅲ.①游戏—介绍—中国—汉、英 Ⅳ.①G898

中国国家版本馆CIP数据核字（2024）第017276号

符号中国：中国传统游戏 CHINESE TRADITIONAL GAMES

编　　著	"符号中国"编写组
策划编辑	沙　平
责任编辑	罗丹阳
英文编辑	邱　械
美术编辑	曹　娜　郑亚超　洪　涛
出版发行	中央民族大学出版社
	北京市海淀区中关村南大街27号　　邮编：100081
	电话：（010）68472815（发行部）　传真：（010）68933757（发行部）
	（010）68932218（总编室）　　　　（010）68932447（办公室）
经销者	全国各地新华书店
印刷厂	北京兴星伟业印刷有限公司
开　　本	787 mm×1092 mm　1/16　印张：8
字　　数	110千字
版　　次	2024年9月第1版　2024年9月第1次印刷
书　　号	ISBN 978-7-5660-2334-6
定　　价	58.00元

版权所有　侵权必究

"符号中国"丛书编委会

唐兰东　巴哈提　杨国华　孟靖朝　赵秀琴

本册编写者

王　慧

前言 Preface

中国传统游戏具有悠久的历史，是华夏文化的重要组成部分。中国学者林语堂曾说过："若不知道人民日常的娱乐方法，便不能认识一个民族。"中国古代劳动人民在用智慧和力量创造物质财富的同时，也创造出了许多能够愉悦身心、锻炼身体、增

Chinese Traditional games, as time-honored entertaining activities, serve as an important part of Chinese culture. A quote from a modern Chinese scholar, Lin Yutang, once described it as, "You cannot understand a nation if you have no idea about the daily entertainment of its people." Apart from creating material wealth with their wisdom and strength, the industrious people in ancient China have also created lots of original games for mental pleasure, physical exercise, and intellectual enhancement. For example, *Cuju* (ancient Chinese soccer), was recognized as the earliest form of football by FIFA in early 2004; Huarong Path Escape, is regarded as one of the world's top three incredible puzzle games; and tangram (seven-piece puzzle), is praised as one of the oldest oriental pastimes by British historian of science Dr. Joseph Needham. These traditional games are not only a precious

强智力的独特游戏。例如，在2004年初被国际足球协会（FIFA）公开确认为世界最早的足球形式的蹴鞠，被视为"世界三大不可思议的智力游戏"之一的华容道和被英国科学史专家李约瑟博士称之为"东方最古老的消遣品之一"的七巧板等。这些传统游戏不仅是中华民族的宝贵财富，也是世界游戏的重要组成部分。

本书介绍了竞技类、民俗类、风雅类、益智类和休闲类这五大类别的中国传统游戏，以帮助大家更好地了解、认识和探究中国传统游戏的魅力。

treasure of the Chinese people, but also an important part of the world games.

This book introduces five major categories of Chinese traditional games: sport games, folk games, elegant games, puzzle games and casual games, for a purpose of helping readers to gain a better understanding of the charm of Chinese traditional games.

目录 Contents

中国传统游戏概述
Overview of Chinese Traditional Games 001

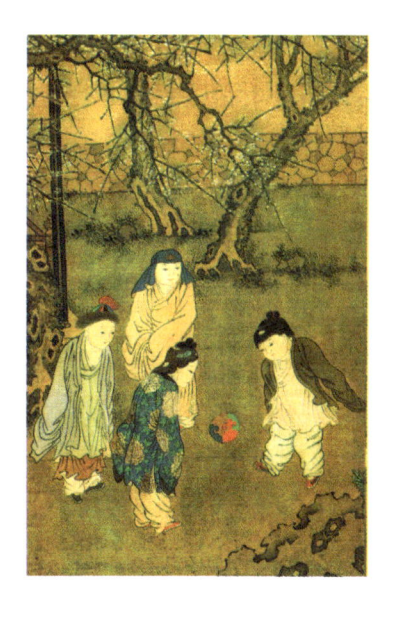

中国传统游戏种类
Categorization of Chinese
Traditional Games 013

竞技类游戏
Sport Games 014

民俗类游戏
Folk Games 039

风雅类游戏
Elegant Games 061

益智类游戏
Puzzle Games 085

休闲类游戏
Casual Games 099

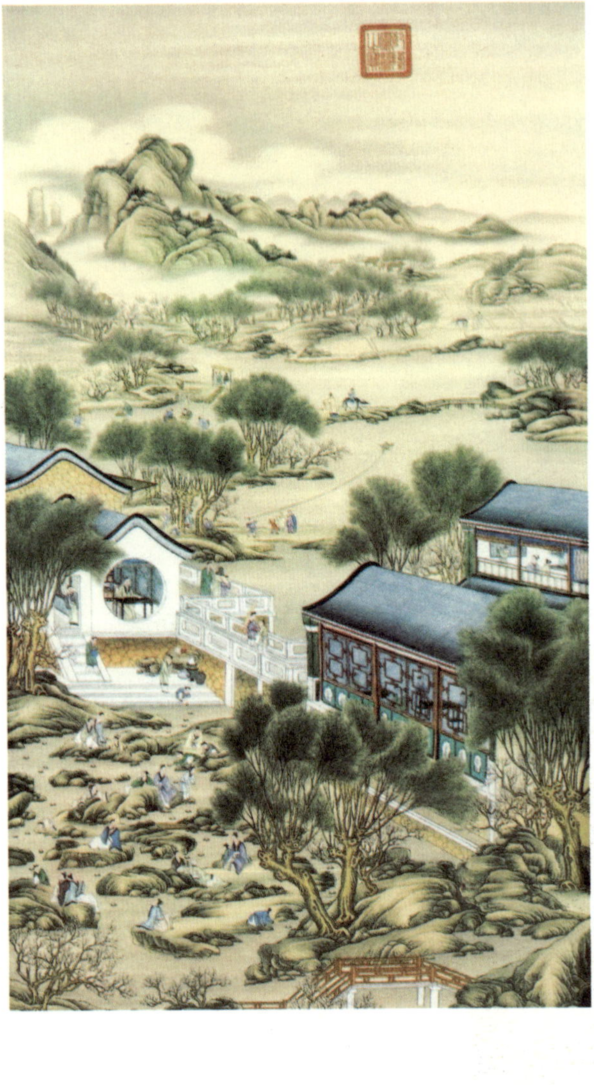

中国传统游戏概述
Overview of Chinese Traditional Games

　　传统游戏是指经过历史的传承，在民间广泛流行的嬉戏和玩耍活动。作为中国传统文化的重要内容，中国传统游戏在一定程度上反映了中国社会发展的历史进程。这些传统游戏由于受社会和经济发展水平的影响，在不同的历史时期呈现出不同的形式特点。按其发展进程大致可以分为原始时期、先秦时期、汉魏时期、唐宋时期和明清时期五个历史阶段。

Traditional games refer to the entertaining activities that have been inherited from generation to generation and that have been enjoying a wide popularity among the folks. As an important part of Chinese traditional culture, Chinese traditional games to some extent reflect the historical process of China's social development. Affected by the level of social and economic developments, these games present different characteristics and forms in different historical periods. Their development process can be roughly divided into five historical periods: the primitive period, period of pre-Qin Dynasty (before 221 B.C.), period of the Han Dynasty (206 B.C.–220 A.D.) and the Wei Dynasty (220–265), period of the Tang Dynasty (618–907) and the Song Dynasty (960–1279), and period of the Ming Dynasty (1368–1644) and the Qing Dynasty (1616–1911).

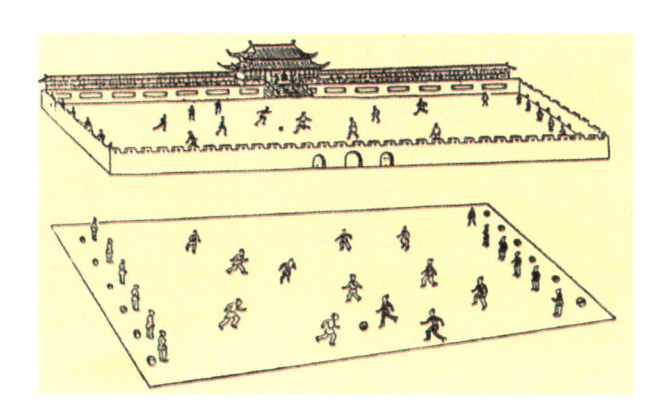

自从有了人类，就产生了游戏，游戏是在人们的日常生活中自然形成的。中国传统游戏的起源最早可以追溯到上古时代，当时还仅仅是人类最原始的娱乐形式。石

- **石球**

石球经过打磨，表面十分光滑，是原始社会时期人们投掷、脚踢的游戏用具。

Stone Ball

After being polished, stone ball has a very smooth surface, which was a tool for people in the primitive society to play throwing and kicking games.

Ever since the emergence of human beings, games have been naturally formed in people's daily lives. The origin of Chinese traditional games can be traced back to ancient times, when they were just the most primitive entertainment for human beings. Stone ball, a spherical natural stone, is considered as China's earliest toy for game, which was originally a hunting tool invented in the middle Paleolithic Period. During hunting, people used strap to string two or three stone balls that were wrapped with hides, and then cast them toward preys, which was a very effective hunting method to entangle the legs of preys. With the emergence of agricultural society and the invention of bow and arrow, stone ball gradually faded away its function as weapon, changing from a hunting tool to a toy for children to kick and play. In the Banpo Village's Yangshao Culture Ruins located

• 射箭

在一万年前的中石器时代，人们发明了弓箭。

Archery

Human invented bow and arrow in the Mesolithic Age about 10,000 years ago.

球被认为是中国最早的游戏玩具，为球形的天然石块，原本是旧石器时代中期发明的一种狩猎工具。在狩猎的时候，人们将两三个用兽皮包裹的石球以皮条连在一起，对准猎物抛出可以很容易缠住猎物的腿部，是一种十分奏效的捕猎方法。随着农业社会的出现和弓箭的发明，石球的武器功能逐渐消失，从狩猎工具变为儿童踢弄、嬉戏的玩具。在陕西西安半坡村仰韶文化遗址，考古学家曾在一个三四岁女孩 in Xi'an of Shaanxi Province, archaeologists found three polished lightweight stone balls and an earthen gyro in the burial of a three-year-old girl.

In the slavery society, the Chinese nation went further toward civilization with rapid development in economy and culture. The period of pre-Qin Dynasty was the primary stage of the development of games. Some simple games began to emerge at that time, and most of them were boorish and primitive, retaining more or less the trace left by the era of primitive hunting and farming. However, along with the progress of handicraft industry, the games with props began to emerge.

Liubo or *Lubo* was an old game prevalent during the period of pre-Qin Dynasty. It was a kind of board game with certain gambling characteristics. According to China's first ancient book about the origin of characters, *Explaining Chinese Characters*, "*Liubo* is a board

的墓葬中发现了三个经过打磨的、形体轻巧的石球，同时出土的还有一枚陶制陀螺。

奴隶制社会时期，中华民族进一步走向文明，经济和文化得以快速发展。先秦时期是游戏发展的初级阶段，一些玩法简单的游戏开始产生。这些游戏大都较为粗犷和原始，多少保留了原始狩猎和原始农业时代的遗风。不过，随着手工业的进步，需要道具的游戏开始出现。

六博是先秦时代非常盛行的一种游戏。这是一种带有一定赌博性质的棋类游戏，又称"陆博"。据中国第一部考究字源的古籍《说文解字》记载："（六博）局戏也，六箸十二棋也。古者乌曹作博。"夏代（约前2070—前1600）时，桀王的臣子乌曹发明了六博，并开始在宫廷和上层社会中流行。《论语》《庄子》《楚辞》《史记》等先秦文献中都有关于六博的记载。到了春秋战国时期，随着经济的发展，六博开始盛行。

春秋战国时期，游戏得到了进一步发展。中国现存最早的编年体史书《左传》中，就记载了鲁国的

game using six chopsticks and twelve chesses. It was an ancestor named Wu Cao that invented it." In the Xia Dynasty (c. 2070 B.C.-1600 B.C.), Wu Cao, an officer of King Jie, invented *Liubo*, which became popular inside the palace and among the upper class. *Liubo* was recorded in *The Analects of Confucius*, *Zhuang Zi*, *The Songs of Chu*, *Records of the Historian* and other pre-Qin literatures. When it came to the time of the Spring and Autumn Period (770 B.C.-476 B.C.) and the Warring States Period (475 B.C.-221 B.C.), such gambling game became more popular thanks to the development of the economy.

In the Spring and Autumn Period to the Warring States Period, the game was further developed. In China's earliest existing chronicle historical records *The Commentary of Zuo*, there is a story about two officers from the State of Lu, Mr. Ji and Mr. Hou, who once played cockfighting for fun. Cockfighting was a game to put together two fierce cocks, and then let them fight with each other by pecking or scratching, so as to create amusement for audience. In order to make the cockfighting more furious and more interesting, and the cocks could win the fight, Mr. Ji clothed his cock with

季氏和郈（hòu）氏两位大夫斗鸡取乐之事。斗鸡是指人们将两只性情凶猛的公鸡放在一起互相啄咬争斗，以此来寻求乐趣的一种游戏。为了使鸡争斗起来更凶猛、更有趣，并且能够斗赢对方，季氏为鸡披上了特制的铁甲，而郈氏则给鸡爪子套上了金属套子。这说明了当时的斗鸡之术已经十分发达。斗鸡游戏不仅在王公贵族中十分盛行，在民间也蔚然成风。据西汉（前206—公元25）刘向编定的史书《战国策·齐策》记述："临淄甚富而实，其民无不吹竽、鼓瑟、击筑、弹琴、斗鸡、走犬、六博、蹴鞠者。"记载中除"斗鸡"外，"走狗""六博""蹴鞠"等也都是当

a special armor, while Mr. Hou wore the claws of his cock with metal gloves. This way of cockfighting shows that the technique of cockfighting at that time has been well-developed. Cockfighting not only enjoyed a good popularity among the nobility, but even the folk were also keen on it. According to *Records of the Warring States: the State of Qi*, Linzi City was so rich and well-off that all of its people were enthusiastic about playing *Yu* (a Chinese traditional wind instrument), *Se* (a 25-stringed plucked instrument), *Zhu* (a 13-stringed plucked instrument) and *Qin* (a 7-stringed plucked instrument), as well as cockfighting, dog racing, *Liubo*, *Taju* (also called *Cuju*, meaning ancient Chinese soccer) and other popular games and activities. In

- 斗鸡画像石（汉）（图片提供：FOTOE）
Stone Relief Carved with Cockfighting (Han Dynasty, 206 B.C.-220 A.D.)

时社会中非常盛行的游戏活动。另外，角抵（摔跤）、拔河、踩高跷、荡秋千、放风筝、赛龙舟等游戏也已经出现。

汉魏时期是中国游戏史上承上启下的重要发展阶段，这一时期在以帝王为首的统治阶层里十分盛行官家游戏，如礼仪烦琐且计数复杂的投壶、格五、弹棋等。在先秦时期就已经出现的蹴鞠，在汉魏时期受到帝王贵族的推崇。为此，他们专门建设了"鞠城"作为比赛场地。鞠城大都挖在地下，这是为了不让球滚得很远，以免追逐起来劳累。西汉著名将军霍去病就喜爱蹴

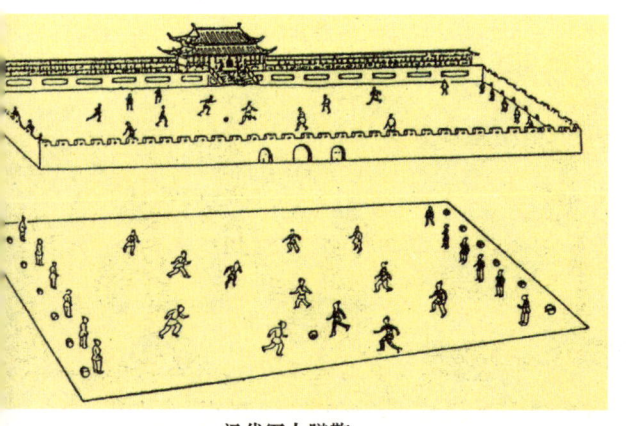

• 汉代军人蹴鞠（图片提供：FOTOE）
Soldiers Playing Ancient Chinese Soccer (Han Dynasty, 206 B.C.-220 A.D.)

addition, games like wrestling, tug of war, stilt walking, swinging, kite flying and loong boat racing have also already emerged at the time.

The period of the Han and Wei dynasties, as a connecting link between the preceding and the following, was an important development stage in the history of Chinese games. The official games were popular among the ruling class led by emperors or kings, such as *Touhu* (pitch-pot, a game of pitching arrows toward a pot), *Gewu* (grid five, an ancient Chinese chess game), flipping chess and other games with complicated etiquettes and calculations. A typical one was *Cuju*, which emerged in the period of pre-Qin Dynasty and became so popular among the imperial nobility during the Han and Wei dynasties that Soccer Towns were specially built as its playing fields. Most of the soccer towns were built under the ground to avoid the soccer rolling too far away as the players might get too tired during chasing. Huo Qubing, a famous general of the Western Han Dynasty, was an enthusiast of ancient Chinese soccer. When he was garrisoning in frontier fortresses, the general often played ancient Chinese soccer with soldiers, which was regarded as a way to

鞠，在守卫边塞时，经常与士兵们一起蹴鞠，以提高士气。在汉代贵族和士大夫中还流行一种雅戏，即被称为"格五"的棋类游戏，主要是靠行棋的技术来战胜对手。而在平民中间则流行一些取材容易、制作方便、简单易行的游戏，如放风筝、角抵、荡秋千等。

唐宋时期游戏的主要特点是普及化和通俗化，出现了许多新型游

• 《营业写真·卖纸鸢》（清）

Picture of Business: Selling Kites (Qing Dynasty, 1616-1911)

boost the morale of soldiers. There was another elegant game popular among the nobles and literati in the Han Dynasty (206 B.C.-220 A.D.), namely grid five, which was a board game played mainly by utilizing tricks. The civilians however were fond of those simple games that were easy to make and play, such as kite flying, wrestling, swing, etc.

The games of the Tang and Song dynasties mainly featured of universalization and popularization, and many new games emerged, such as polo, Chinese chess, *Yezixi* (leaves play, a Chinese traditional card game), and so on. Affected by the then feudal policy of Sharing Happiness with People, the official games, which were originally in vogue during the period of the Han and Wei dynasties, gradually walked into the folk, becoming well-received entertaining activities for ordinary people. Wrestling, for example, was not only popular inside the palace, but also prevalent in the folk, where many wrestling communities and experts emerged. According to *Records of Wrestling* written by Diao Luzi in the Northern Song Dynasty, "The townspeople in recent times would hold wrestling games on each lunar January 15th, and they were extremely

● 象棋（清）
Chinese Chess (Qing Dynasty, 1616-1911)

戏，例如打马球、象棋、叶子戏等。受当时封建统治阶级"与民同乐"政策的影响，原本在汉魏时期大放异彩的官家游戏逐渐走向民间，成了普通民众喜闻乐见的娱乐活动。例如，摔跤不仅在宫廷盛行，在民间也涌现出了许多摔跤社团和摔跤能手。北宋（960—1127）调露子所著的《角力记》载："近代以来，都邑百姓每至正月十五日，做角抵戏，递相夸竞，至于糜费财力。"有些人甚至为此而废寝忘食，到了痴迷的程度。每逢农历五月，江南的民众都要举行划龙舟

crazy about comparing with each other during the games, causing a lot of waste of money." Some people became so obsessed with the game that even forgetting all about food and sleep. In each lunar May, people living in regions South of the Yangtze River would hold loong boat racings and wrestling games. Funds would be raised to buy rewards for these games, and the winner wearing the rewarded colored silks was allowed to ride a horse to show off all over the whole town, where people had all turned out to watch the games.

During the period of the Ming Dynasty and the Qing Dynasty, which

比赛，同时，也聚集起来进行相扑（即摔跤）大会。人们募集比赛经费用以购买奖品，万人空巷去看比赛，获胜者身披彩绸骑着马游街炫耀。

明清时期是中国封建社会的末期，传统游戏虽然种类齐全，但创新不多。蹴鞠、摔跤、荡秋千、放风筝、斗蟋蟀等游戏依旧盛行。斗蟋蟀也称"斗促织""斗蛐蛐"，就是以蟋蟀相斗为戏，相传始于唐

- 蟋蟀罐（明）
Cricket Cans(Ming Dynasty,1368-1644)

was the end of China's feudal society, the traditional games were of little innovation though the categories had come to a full range. Games like ancient Chinese soccer, wrestling, swing, kite flying and cricket fighting were still in vogue during this period. Cricket fighting, known as *Doucuzhi* or *Douququ* in Chinese, was a game to let crickets fight with each other. It was said that this game dated from the Tianbao Period (742-756) in the Tang Dynasty and became popular in the Ming Dynasty. It was recorded in the book *History of the Song Dynasty: Biography of Jia Sidao*, and there was a ballad saying that Emperor Xuanzong was a fan of cricket fighting. In the Qing Dynasty, cricket fighting become more and more fastidious. According to *Records of Qingjia* written by Gu Lu in the Qing Dynasty, "People raised and trained crickets to fight for gambling during about the White Dew (15th solar term), which was called *Qiuxing* (Autumn Fun) and commonly known as *Douzhuanji* (cricket fighting); and players carrying crickets cages would gather in crowds, calling their crickets as general." Moreover, rope skipping, called Skipping *Tiaobaisuo* (Hundred Ropes) in ancient

代天宝年间。《宋史·贾似道传》中也有斗蟋蟀的记载。斗蟋蟀在明代（1368—1644）尤为盛行，有"蟋蟀瞿瞿叫，宣德皇帝要"的民谣。到了清代（1616—1911），斗蟋蟀越发考究，清人顾禄的《清嘉录》载："白露前后，驯养蟋蟀，以为赌斗之乐，谓之秋兴，俗名斗赚绩。提笼相望，结队成群，呼其虫为将军。"另有跳绳，古称"跳百索"，在明清时期非常流行。明

times, was also very popular in the folk during the period of the Ming Dynasty and the Qing Dynasty. According to *Jottings of Wanshu* written by Shen Bang in the Ming Dynasty, "*Tiaobaisuo* was a game that two children held the two ends of a rope about 3 meters long and swung it fast to make it look as if there were 100 ropes; at this time, other children jumped into the swinging rope one by one, and those who could skip out from it would win while those who touched the rope would break the rules

• 谢环《杏园雅集图》【局部】（明）
Painting of Gathering for Elegant Games in Apricot Garden, by Xie Huan (Ming Dynasty, 1368-1644) [Part]

人沈榜在《宛署杂记》载："以长绳丈许，两儿对牵，飞摆不定，令难疑视，若百索然，其实一索也。群儿乘其动时轮跳其上，以能过者为胜，否或为索所绊，听掌绳者以击之为罪，名曰：跳百索。"此外，棋牌类游戏的发展也十分迅速，以象棋和围棋最为突出，涌现出了一大批棋艺精湛的高手。例如，明代象棋高手李开先、围棋国手过百龄及清代围棋国手范西屏等。

and lose the game." In addition, board games experienced a rapid development at this period. The most prominent ones were Chinese chess and the game of Go, and a large number of exquisite chess masters emerged in the two games, such as Chinese chess master Li Kaixian and national Go player Guo Bailing in the Ming Dynasty, national Go player Fan Xiping in the Qing Dynasty, etc.

Chinese traditional games have lots of categories, and the emergence and development of each category has its own

中国传统游戏的种类很多，各种类型的游戏出现的时间与发展的过程都有自身的特定轨迹。各地还流传着许多具有浓厚生活情趣、风格各异的民间游戏。其中有相当一部分传统游戏流传至今，仍然在丰富着中国人的生活。

particular track. Meanwhile, many folk games with strong life tastes and different styles have spread across a lot of places. Quite a number of these traditional games spread up to now and is still creating joys to the lives of Chinese people.

- 瓷围棋盘（隋）
Ceramic Chessboard(Sui Dynasty,581-618)

中国传统游戏种类
Categorization of Chinese Traditional Games

中国传统游戏历史悠久、种类繁多。本章根据娱乐性质将其分为竞技类、民俗类、风雅类、益智类和休闲类五大类，并选取各类别中最具代表性的游戏，详细介绍其历史、现状与玩法。

Due to their long history, Chinese traditional games contain wide categories. This chapter, based on their nature of entertainment, divides them into five categories of sport games, folk games, elegant games, puzzle games and casual games, and selects the most representative ones from each category to have a detailed introduction about their history, current situation and playing procedures.

> 竞技类游戏

蹴鞠

蹴鞠,又名"蹋鞠""蹴球"。"蹴"即用脚踢,"鞠"即皮制的球。蹴鞠起源于战国时期,最早记载于《史记·苏秦列传》。在当时的齐国都城临淄,斗鸡和蹴鞠已经成为普通百姓的竞技比赛项目。

汉代(前206—公元220)时,人们将蹴鞠视为"治国习武"之道,军营中经常举行蹴鞠比赛,用以锻炼士兵的体质。汉代桓宽在《盐铁论》中写道:"康庄驰逐,穷巷蹴鞠。"可以看出在当时平民多以蹴鞠为乐。据《汉书》记载,汉高祖刘邦就经常在宫中举行以斗鸡和蹴鞠比赛为内容的"鸡鞠之会"。

> Sport Games

Ancient Chinese Soccer

Ancient Chinese soccer is known as *Cuju*, *Taju* or *Juqiu* in Chinese. *Cu* means kicking and *Ju* means a leather ball. The game originated in the Warring States Period, and the earliest record about it can be found in *Records of the Historian, Collected Biographies of Suqin*. At the time, cockfighting and ancient Chinese soccer were treated as sporting events for common people of Linzi, capital of the State of Qi.

In the Han Dynasty, as ancient Chinese soccer was regarded as a way of practicing martial arts to protect the country, competitions of ancient Chinese soccer were frequently held to train the physical fitness of soldiers. According to *Debates on Salt and Iron* written by Huan Kuan in the Han Dynasty, people were so

• 蹴鞠画像石（汉）
Stone Relief Carved with Ancient Chinese Soccer Game
(Han Dynasty, 206 B.C.-220 A.D.)

唐宋时期是蹴鞠发展的鼎盛时期，既有两三人的小型蹴鞠表演，也有超过百人的大型竞技比赛。这一时期，蹴鞠不仅是帝王、贵族所钟爱的游戏，同时还深受普通百姓的喜爱。唐代（618—907）时，宫廷中经常出现"球不离足，足不离球"的情景，并出现了具有表演性质的女子蹴鞠。此时，蹴鞠制作工

keen on ancient Chinese soccer that you could find players everywhere, which meant that both the rich and the populace were fans of ancient Chinese soccer. Also, as recorded in *History of the Han Dynasty*, Liu Bang (Emperor Gaozu of the Han Dynasty) once often held games of cockfighting and ancient Chinese soccer in palace, namely the Meeting of Cock and Soccer.

● 苏汉臣《宋太祖蹴鞠图》（北宋）

此图描绘的是宋太祖赵匡胤与其弟赵匡义、近臣赵普等人蹴鞠的情景。

Painting of the Song Dynasty's Emperor Taizu Playing Ancient Chinese Soccer, by Su Hanchen (Northern Song Dynasty, 960-1127)

The painting depicts the scene that Zhao Kuangyin, Emperor Taizu of the Song Dynasty, is playing ancient Chinese soccer with his brother Zhao Kuangyi, his courtier Zhao Pu and some other attendants.

艺有了很大改进：一是将原有的两块皮壳增加至八块，使其形状更加规范；二是将皮球从使用动物毛发作为填充物改为使用动物尿脬，使之成为充气的球，重量更轻。宋代时，人们在寒食节这一天进行蹴鞠比赛。南宋词人陆游在其诗作《春

The period of the Tang Dynasty and the Song Dynasty was the heyday of ancient Chinese soccer's development, when there were small shows with two or three performers and big sport competitions with more than one hundred players. During this period, ancient Chinese soccer was not only the favorite game for emperors and nobles, but also a well-received entertaining activity for ordinary people. In the Tang Dynasty, there in palace often appeared the scene where players were scrambling for soccer on the field fiercely. Meanwhile, female soccer with a performing characteristic also emerged. At this point, the craftsmanship of ancient Chinese soccer showed great improvements: firstly, the number of leather pieces was added from the original two to eight pieces, making a more normative shape; secondly, the padding inside the ball was changed from animal hair to animal bladders, producing a lighter inflatable ball. In the Song Dynasty, people hold games of ancient Chinese soccer on the day of Cold Food Festival. The poem *Sentiments in Late Spring*, which was written by poet Lu You in the Southern Song Dynasty, says that, "Thousands of families celebrate Cold Food Festival in Liangzhou. Millions of

晚感事》中写道："寒食梁州十万家，秋千蹴鞠尚豪华。"据《宋史》记载，凡是朝廷的盛大宴会都会有蹴鞠表演。南宋时，在民间各地出现了名为"齐云社"的蹴鞠社团，其中以临安（今浙江杭州）的齐云社实力最强。"齐云"就是将"鞠"踢得高入云端的意思。

元明时期，蹴鞠活动也十分兴盛，还开展了女子蹴鞠活动。元代戏曲家关汉卿创作了以齐云社女蹴鞠艺人为题的散曲作品《女校尉》（校尉是齐云社蹴鞠艺人中的最高等级）。明代时，为了增加蹴鞠

people play games of ancient Chinese soccer and swing all over the city." According to the *History of the Song Dynasty*, the show of ancient Chinese soccer was a routine for all the official gaudies. In the Southern Song Dynasty (1127-1279), many ancient Chinese soccer associations named *Qiyun* (Clouds High) sprang up in the folk in lots of places, and the most influential one was that in Lin'an (current Hangzhou City, Zhejiang Province). The word Clouds High means to kick the soccer as high as clouds.

During the period of the Yuan Dynasty (1206-1368) and the Ming Dynasty (1368-1644), ancient Chinese

• **元代蹴鞠** （图片提供：FOTOE）
Ancient Chinese Soccer (Yuan Dynasty, 1206-1368)

苏汉臣《长春百子图》【局部】（北宋）
Painting of One Hundred Children in Eternal Spring, by Su Hanchen (Northern Song Dynasty, 960-1127)[Part]

的观赏性，于是从杂技行业中选取技艺高超者来进行蹴鞠表演。清代时，关于蹴鞠的记载已寥寥无几，蹴鞠竞技逐渐消失。如今，足球取代了古代蹴鞠，并且成为世界上最受欢迎的球类运动之一。

古代蹴鞠的竞技形式主要有直接对抗、间接对抗和白打三种。

直接对抗是汉代蹴鞠的主要竞

soccer was also an activity in vogue, especially female soccer game. Guan Hanqing, a drama composer and play writer of the Yuan Dynasty, created a verse about female artists who played ancient Chinese soccer in Clouds High, namely *Female Captain* (captain was the highest official title for artist of ancient Chinese soccer in Clouds High). In the Ming Dynasty, in order to increase its spectacularity, highly skilled performers were selected from acrobatic troupe to play ancient Chinese soccer. In the Qing Dynasty, little records about ancient Chinese soccer were found, and this sport game gradually disappeared. Nowadays, modern soccer has replaced ancient Chinese soccer and become one of the most popular ball games in the world.

In ancient times, there were three ways to play ancient Chinese soccer: direct confrontation, indirect confrontation and freestyle.

Direct confrontation was the way mainly used to play ancient Chinese soccer in the Han Dynasty. The game was played within a soccer town surrounded by short walls, and each team had 12 players, who should protect their own goal and invade the opposite goal. The team got more goals within a fixed time

技形式。蹴鞠比赛在设有短墙的鞠城内进行，蹴鞠双方球员各十二名，两边队员相对进攻，要分别守护自己场地后方的球门，在规定的时间内以进球多者为胜。在直接对抗的蹴鞠比赛中，肢体对抗十分频繁。

间接对抗是唐代蹴鞠的主要竞技形式。间接对抗与直接对抗在形式上的差别主要为球门数由两个变为一个，环门位置从球场后方改为球场中央，双方球员没有肢体接触。间接对抗的蹴鞠比赛主要用于为朝廷宴乐和外交礼仪竞赛表演。

白打即无球门的散踢形式，人数从一人至十人皆可，唐代时期就已出现，是历时最久、流行最为广泛的蹴鞠竞技形式。蹴鞠者主要比拼花样和技巧，有多种踢球动作，例如"转乾坤""燕归巢""斜插花""风摆荷""双肩背月""拐子流星"等。

would win the game. By using such way of direct confrontation, it was very often to see physical contact during the game.

Indirect confrontation was the way mainly used to play ancient Chinese soccer in the Tang Dynasty. The major differences between indirect confrontation and direct confrontation were that the number of goals was changed from two to one, whose location was changed from the rear to the middle of the field. Besides, there was no physical contact in such way of playing. Ancient Chinese soccer played in the way of indirect confrontation was mainly treated as a sport performance for imperial banquets and diplomatic ceremonies.

Freestyle referred to the way that the goal was unnecessary and that the number of players could be one to ten. Appeared in the Tang Dynasty, the freestyle way was the earliest and the most widespread way of playing ancient Chinese soccer. In this way, what the players competed were the skills and gestures to kick the ball, such as *Zhuan Qiankun* (moving the heaven), *Yan Guichao* (coming-back swallow), *Xiecha Hua* (obliquely-inserted flower), *Feng Baihe* (wind-swing lotus), *Shuangjian Beiyue* (shoulders-holding moon), *Guaizi Liuxing* (cripple meteor), etc.

打马球

打马球，又称"击鞠""击球"，是一种人骑在马上用长柄球杖击球的竞技游戏，多见于古代宫廷、贵族及军营当中。

目前，关于马球出现的确切年代还没有定论。唐代初期，打马球就已经在中国出现。唐代时马术发达，打马球在宫廷和军营中逐渐

- 打马球俑（唐）（图片提供：FOTOE）
Polo Tomb Figure (Tang Dynasty, 618-907)

Polo

Polo, also known as *Jiju* or *Jiqiu* (both mean ball hitting), was a sport game to hit ball with a long-handled stick while riding a horse, which was common in ancient palaces, noble mansions as well as barracks.

Currently, the exact date for polo's appearance has not yet been conclusive. The early Tang Dynasty, playing polo emerged in China. Due to the well-developed equestrianism in the Tang Dynasty, polo gradually prevailed in palaces and barracks. Li Longji, Emperor Xuanzong of the Tang Dynasty) was very good at playing polo, and he often played the game with maids and eunuchs. In 747, he specially issued an edict to list polo as a training subject for barracks. Meanwhile, female polo of a more ornamental value also emerged during this period.

In the Song Dynasty, polo was still popular in palaces and female polo experienced the fastest development. At that time, women had to be capable of horseback riding and poetry reciting before they were allowed to learn polo. Lady Huarui, a poet in the Song Dynasty, once wrote in her poem *Words*

墓葬壁画《打马球图》（唐）（图片提供：FOTOE）
Tomb Mural: *Polo Game* (Tang Dynasty, 618-907)

盛行。唐玄宗李隆基十分擅长打马球，经常与宫女、宦官们一起竞技。公元747年，唐玄宗还专门颁发诏书，将马球列为军营的训练科目。同时，更具观赏性的女子马球也已产生。

宋代时，打马球在宫廷中仍旧十分流行，以女子马球发展最快。当时，会骑马且能吟诗的女子才可学习打马球。宋代花蕊夫人在其诗作《宫词》中写道："自教宫娥学 *of Palace* that, "Self-taught palace maids lean how to play polo, their waists look so narrow and soft when they step onto the jade saddles for the first time." During the reign of Zhao Ji (Emperor Huizong of Song Dynasty), a female polo team was set up in palace and imperial concubine Cui Shuyi was appointed as the captain while extreme gorgeous dresses were granted to the team players and horses.

Since the period of the Ming Dynasty and the Qing Dynasty, polo in

- **丁观鹏《唐明皇击鞠图》【局部】（清）**

此图描述了唐明皇（即唐玄宗）在宫廷内打马球的情景。当时，球门高约一丈（约三米），球门木柱加以木雕装饰，底部设石莲花座，上方插有绣旗。

Painting of Emperor Ming of the Tang Dynasty Playing Polo, by Ding Guanpeng [Part] (Qing Dynasty, 1616-1911)

The painting depicts the scene that Emperor Ming of the Tang Dynasty, namely Emperor Xuanzong of the Tang Dynasty, is playing polo in palace. At the time, the goal, about three meters high, had two poles decorated with carvings, a stone lotus-shaped base, and a roof inserted with embroidered flags.

打球，玉鞍初跨柳腰柔。"宋徽宗赵佶在位期间，在皇宫中成立了女子马球队，并由贵妃崔淑仪亲自担任队长，球员的服饰和马匹的装束都十分华丽。

从明清时期开始，打马球在中国民间已不多见。如今，打马球被视作一种高尚的体育运动，在世界范围内流行开来。

打马球所用的球杖和马球都选用坚硬的木质材料。马球球杖长约数尺，底端弯曲如偃月，杖柄笔

the Chinese folk has become a rare game. Today, polo is regarded as a noble sport that is spread all over the world.

The stick and ball of polo are made of hard wood materials. The stick, about one meter long, has a crescent-moon bottom and a straight handle. Engraved with various patterns, it was called Engraving Stick or Moon Stick by ancient literati. The ball was hollow in a size as large as a fist. As its outer surface could be decorated with a variety of colors or engravings, the ball often appeared in literary works in the name

直，常雕刻有各种花样，古代文人称之为"画杖"或"月杖"。马球大小如拳头一般，中空，因其外部常装饰有各种色彩或雕刻纹饰，故在文学作品中多以"彩球""七宝球""画球"等名称出现。

在古代，打马球比赛时分作两队，有专门的比赛球场。场地分为泥地、草地和沙地三种：泥地球场的泥土要经过细筛，夯打碾压，有时还要掺入适当的牛油，以防止比赛时尘土飞扬。草地球场多选用天然草场。沙地球场多为雨天比赛时使用。双方场地后方各设一球门，

of Colored Ball, Seven-treasures Ball, Engraving ball, etc.

In ancient times, there were two teams in a polo game, and there were specialized playing fields, which could be divided into three types of clay field, grass field and sand field. The clay used for clay field must be filtered and ground, and sometimes even be mixed with appropriate beef tallow, so as to prevent the blowing dust during the game. The grass field usually was set on natural meadows while the sand field was mainly used in rainy days. Each team had a goal on the rear part of their side, and the ball hole was set in the bottom of the goal.

• 打马球纹铜镜（唐）
Bronze Mirror with Polo Playing Pattern (Tang Dynasty, 618-907)

球洞在球门底端，最先打进的球被称为"头筹"，在宫廷比赛中头筹只能由皇帝打入。双方以在规定的时间内进球的多少来判断胜负。

摔跤

摔跤，又称"角力""角抵""相扑"或"手搏"等，是两人徒手互搏，用各种技巧、方法摔倒对手的竞技游戏。

在原始社会时期，人们在争夺食物或者部族斗争中徒手互搏时，传统的摔跤就已产生。周代（前1046—前256）时，摔跤称作"角力"，同射箭一起作为训练科目在军营中出现。在战国时期的《礼

● 孩童摔跤雕塑 （图片提供：微图）
Kids Wrestling Sculpture

The first score was called Head Start, which was exclusive to the emperor during the games played in palace. The team that got more scores within a stipulated time would be the winner of the game.

Wrestling

Wrestling, also known as *Jiaoli*, *Jiaodi*, *Xiangpu* or *Shoubo* in Chinese, is a sport game that two players combat with each other bare-handedly by using a variety of skills and methods to tumble the opponent.

In primitive society, people combated with each other bare-handedly during food scrambling or tribe fighting, which was the prototype of the traditional wrestling game. In the Zhou Dynasty (1046 B.C.-256 B.C.), wrestling was called *Jiaoli*, and the same as archery, it was listed as a training subject for barracks. According to the relevant records in *Book of Rites: Yue Ling* of the Warring States period, "On the first lunar month of winter…the Emperor ordered generals to teach him martial artists, including *Jiaoli* (archery and wrestling)." From the Spring and Autumn Period to the Warring States

- 绢画摔跤（汉）（图片提供：FOTOE）

此绢画出土于山东临沂地区金雀山汉墓，上有三名男子，中间的为裁判，左右挽着袖子互相对视的为摔跤手。

Silk Painting of Wrestling (Han Dynasty, 206 B.C.-220 A.D.)

This silk painting was unearthed from the tombs of the Han Dynasty on Jinque Mountain in Linyi region of Shandong Province. There are three men on the painting: the one in the middle is referee and the other two staring into each other on two sides with sleeves rolled up are wresters.

记·月令》中有相关记载："孟冬之月……天子乃命将帅讲武，习射御、角力。"春秋战国时期，摔跤逐渐从军事训练手段演变成了具有娱乐表演性质的竞技游戏。

秦汉时期，摔跤者的头上顶着牛角，所以摔跤又被称作"角抵"，是当时宫廷中的主要娱乐项

Period, wrestling gradually evolved from a means of military training into a sport game with characteristic of entertaining performance.

In the Qin Dynasty (221 B.C.-206 B.C.) and the Han Dynasty(206 B.C.-220 A.D.), wrestlers needed to wear ox horns, so wrestling was also known as *Jiaodi* (*Jiao* means horn and *Di* means

• 《塞宴四事图》（清）
Painting of Four Performances in Frontier Banquet (Qing Dynasty, 1616-1911)

目。当时，摔跤在民间已十分盛行。东汉史学家班固撰写的《汉书》中记载："（元封）三年春，作角抵戏，三百里内皆来观。"描述的是公元前108年，在京城举办的包括摔跤比赛在内的娱乐表演，吸引了方圆三百里内的人前来观看。据史料记载，此时的摔跤比赛中已出现裁判，胜负需由裁判决定。

南北朝至南宋时期，摔跤又被称作"相扑"。唐代时，摔跤活动

heading against), which was the main entertainment in palace at that time. Meanwhile, wrestling was also very popular among the folks. Ban Gu, a historian of the Eastern Han Dynasty (25-220), once wrote in his book *History of Han Dynasty* that, "In 108, the capital city held entertaining performances that included *Jiaodi* (wrestling), which attracted people even three hundred miles far way." And according to historical records, the game of wrestling at this

十分活跃，元宵节和中元节时都要举行摔跤比赛。唐代末年，朝廷还专门开设了官办的"相扑棚"，在民间广泛收罗和训练摔跤能手。在朝会、宴聚、祭祀等活动中，入选相扑棚的"相扑人"都要进行摔跤表演。

宋代时，宫廷摔跤十分盛行，为王公贵族们进行表演的专业摔跤手被称作"内等子"。在民间也出现了一些摔跤社团，名为"角抵社"。北宋《角力记》一书，是中国现存最早的摔跤专著，记载了从春秋战国到五代十国的摔跤历史。

明清时期，摔跤被朝廷视作提高军事作战水平的训练手段。清代时，皇帝大力提倡摔跤活动，康熙皇帝曾在黑龙江木兰举办宴会与蒙古部落进行联欢，摔跤是当时重要的表演项目。朝廷还专门设立了善扑营，广泛收罗摔跤能手，每逢宴会都要进行表演或比赛。清代末年，传统摔跤术已达到相当高的水平。在满语中，摔跤称作"布库"。当时，食俸禄的摔跤手叫"官跤"或"官腿"，民间业余摔跤手则称"私跤"或"私练"。

time had contained a referee, who would decide which player could win the game.

From the Northern and Southern dynasties (420-589) to the Southern Song Dynasty (1127-1279), wrestling was also known as *Xiangpu*. In the Tang Dynasty, wrestling activities were very active, and wrestling games were a must on both the Lantern Festival and Ghost Festival. During the late Tang Dynasty, the government specially set up a *Xiangpu Peng* (government-run Wrestling Shed) to enlist and train extensively in the folk wrestling experts. During activities like gatherings, banquets and worships, the *Xiangpu Ren* (Wrestler) selected into Wrestling Shed would have a wrestling show.

In the Song Dynasty, wrestling was very prevalent in palace, and the professional wrestlers performing for the nobility were called *Neidengzi*. What's more, some wrestling communities called *Jiaodi* Associations also appeared among the folks. The book *Records of Wrestling of the Northern Song Dynasty* is China's earliest existing wrestling monograph, documenting the history of wrestling from the Spring and Autumn Period to the Warring States Period to Five dynasties and Ten states (907-960).

陶相扑俑（金）（图片提供：FOTOE）
Clay Tomb Figures of Wrestlers (Jin Dynasty, 1115-1234)

During the period of the Ming Dynasty and the Qing Dynasty, wrestling was regarded as a training means to improve the level of military operations. In the Qing Dynasty, wrestling activities were greatly promoted by emperors. When Emperor Kangxi held the banquet in Mulan of Heilongjiang Province to entertain Mongolian tribes, wrestling was one of the important performances. The government also set up a special wrestling-master battalion to collect widely wrestling experts, who would have performances or games during each banquet. In the late Qing Dynasty, traditional wrestling reached a quite high level. In Manchu language, wrestling was called *Buku*. At that time, wrestlers living on official salary were called *Guanjiao* (Official Wrestler) or *Guantui* (Official Leg) while amateur wrestlers were called *Sijiao* (Private Wrestler) or *Silian* (Private Trainer).

Today, the Chinese people's wrestling skills have reached a very high level. Wrestling has become not only a game for people to play for entertainment, but also a sport popular all over the world.

如今，中国人的摔跤技术已经达到相当高的水平，摔跤不仅是人们日常的竞技、娱乐的游戏项目，也是在世界范围内十分受欢迎的体育运动。

在古代，摔跤没有固定的场地和严格的时间限制，摔跤手要赤手空拳上阵，不能携带任何兵器，采取一对一的竞技方式，直到一方摔倒在地为止。在汉代时，摔跤就已经出现了两种形式：一是一手抱对方的腰，另一手扳对方的腿；二是没有固定形式，可使击、打、摔、拿等多种动作。由于摔跤是一场力量的比拼，因此在古代摔跤场上常有负伤、死亡的情况发生。

In ancient times, wrestling had no fixed playing field or strict time limit, and wrestlers had to be unarmed to have a one-to-one combat to fall down the opponent. In the Han Dynasty, wrestling appeared with two playing ways: one way is to hold the opponent's waist with one hand while wrenching the opponent's leg with the other hand; another way is free to use beating, hitting, stumbling, holding and other actions, without any fixed limitations. As a contest of strength, the game of wrestling often caused wounds or death in ancient times.

- 瓷器摔跤娃娃（清）（图片提供：微图）
Porcelain Wrestling Babies (Qing Dynasty, 1616-1911)

蒙古族摔跤

　　射箭、骑马和摔跤是蒙古族男子必须掌握的三项竞技能力，也是蒙古族那达慕大会上的固定比赛形式。那达慕大会是蒙古族的盛大集会，在那达慕大会上取胜的摔跤手，将被视作勇士。

　　蒙古族摔跤有独特的服装、规则和方法。蒙古族摔跤手要身穿专业的摔跤服"昭德格"。在比赛开始前，要由蒙古族歌手演唱蒙古长调《摔跤手歌》，为摔跤比赛助兴。然后，摔跤手才挥舞着手臂、跳着鹰舞入场，按照顺时针的方向绕着场地旋转一圈。当裁判发令后，双方互相行礼，然后正式开始比赛。在摔跤的过程中，摔跤手可以使用捉、拉、扯、推、压等动作，但是不能抱腿、打脸，以及背后暗算等。

Mongolian Wrestling

Archery, equestrianism and wrestling are three sporting abilities that Mongolian men must master and three competing items that must be held on Mongolian Nadam, a grand gathering of the Mongolian. Wrestlers who won the games during Nadam would be treated as warriors, obtaining supreme honors.

　　Mongolian wrestling has unique costumes, rules and techniques. Mongolian wrestlers need to dress in professional wrestling costume named *Zhaodege*. Before the game of wrestling, a Mongolian long tune named *Song of Wrestlers* is sung by Mongolian singers to cheer up the game. Then, wrestlers walk onto the field by waving arms and performing eagle dance to circle the field clockwise. After the referee gives an order to start, the two wrestlers salute each other and start the game. In the process of wrestling, wrestlers can use catching, pulling, tearing, pushing, pressing and other actions, but leg holding, face hitting or sneak attacks are now allowed.

坎肩：由牛皮、鹿皮等制作而成，肩上镶有银质或铜质的泡钉。

Waistcoat: It is made by cowhide, deerskin or other materials; beset with silver or copper bubble-shaped nails.

江嘎：这种彩色布条是摔跤手在比赛中获得过奖项的标志。

Jiangga: It is a kind of colored cloth strip meaning that a wrestler once was awarded in the game.

套裤：由多种颜色的绸缎制作而成，宽松多褶，绣有各种吉祥图案。

Overalls: Overalls are made by silks of a various colors; loose, comfortable and pleated; embroidered with all kinds of auspicious patterns.

马靴
Riding Boots

- **蒙古族摔跤**（图片提供：FOTOE）
摔跤服上常绣有龙、鸟、花朵等吉祥图案，颜色鲜艳。
Mongolian Wrestling
The wrestling costume usually is embroidered with loongs, birds, flowers and other bright and colored auspicious patterns.

拔河

　　拔河，早在春秋时期就已经产生，是一种用绳索互相牵拉的竞技游戏。在唐代之前，拔河被称作"牵钩""钩强"或"施钩"。

　　战国时期的典籍《墨子·鲁问》中记载："公输子自鲁南游楚，焉始为舟战之器。"钩强是由中国土木工匠的祖师爷公输子（即鲁班）发明的，是当时楚国水军作战时的武器。当敌人后退时，可用钩强钩住其所乘船只防止其逃脱并消灭之。之后，施钩从水军作战时必备的军事技能发展到陆地上的训练，并逐渐流传至民间。南朝梁（502—557）的宗懔在《荆楚岁时记》中写道："施钩之戏，以绠作篾缆相罥，绵亘数里，鸣鼓牵之。"在当时的荆楚地区（今湖北襄阳一带），人们用竹篾制作的绳子相互牵引、推拉，在鼓声的鼓动下，施钩的队伍绵延好几百米。

　　"拔河"一词最早出现在唐代封演的《封氏闻见记》一书中。唐代时，人们使用大麻绁（一种粗麻绳）代替了竹篾绳索，绳长已达到四五十丈（约合150米）。因以

Tug of War

Tug of war (*Bahe*), which emerged as early as in the Spring and Autumn Period, is a sport game to let two teams pull against each other on a rope. Before the Tang Dynasty, tug of war was known as *Qiangou* (Hook Pulling), *Gouqiang* (Strong Hook) or *Shigou* (Hook Applying).

　　The ancient book *Mo Zi: Questions of Lu* of the Warring States Period once recorded that: When Gong Shuzi traveled from south of the State of Lu to the State of Chu, he invented inadvertently an effective tool for sea battles. Gong Shuzi (i.e. Lu Ban), the earliest ancestor of China's architectural engineers, invented the Strong Hook, which was a military weapon for the navy of the State of Chu. If the enemy wanted to withdraw, the Strong Hook could be used to grapple their ships, so as to prevent their escaping and annihilate them completely. Later, the Hook Applying as a required military skill for ship wars evolved into land training and gradually spread into the folk. According to *Festivals and Traditions of Jingchu People* written by Zong Lin in the Liang Dynasty, people in Jingchu area (today's Xiangyang City,

粗麻绳中间位置插旗为界，旗杆两边的地面上各画上一条竖线，作为"河"界线，故名"拔河"。旗两边的绳索上系有上百条小绳索，拔河者可将其拴挂在身上。在锣鼓声响起后，上百名拔河者相互牵拉、比拼力气，直到一方把另一方拽过河界线。拔河比赛常在清明节、元宵节等传统节日时进行。

明清时期，拔河仍旧是民间最为常见的游戏项目。在京城的街

Hubei Province) at the time used bamboo strips to make ropes for tugging and pulling, and at the instigation of drums, the line of Hook Applying could stretch about several hundred meters long.

The word *Bahe* (tug of war; *Ba* means tugging and *He* refers river) first appeared in Feng Yan's *Daily Records of Mr. Feng* in the Tang Dynasty. At the time, the rope made of bamboo strips was replaced by manila rope, which could be about 150 meters long. The game was called *Bahe* in that a flag was inserted in the middle of the manila rope to serve as the bound, and that two straight lines were drawn on the ground of the two sides of the flag pole to serve as the boundaries of a river. On the two sides of the manila rope, there were hundreds of small ropes, which could be fastened on the bodies of tug-of-war players. After the sound of gong or drum, hundreds of tug-of-war players would pull against each other to compete which team was stronger, until one team pulled the other team across the river boundary. Tug of war was often played on Pure Brightness Festival, Lantern Festival and other traditional festivals.

During the Ming Dynasty and the Qing Dynasty, tug of war was still the

● 母子一起拔河（图片提供：微图）
Mother and Son in the Tug of War

儿童拔河雕塑（图片提供：微图）
The Children's Sculpture in the Tug of War

头，常出现两个小孩相对站立，用一根绳索对拉比拼力气的拔河情景。现在，在一些节日、团体活动中，操作简单的拔河游戏是人们最为喜欢的竞技游戏之一。

踢毽子

踢毽子，又称"攒花""打鸡"，是一种用腿、脚踢打毽子的游戏。根据史料和考古证实，踢毽子早在汉代就已经出现。1913年，在山东济宁喻北屯张村的东汉墓葬中出土了绘有八人踢毽子的画像石。唐代僧人释道宣所撰写的

most common game in the folk. In the streets of the capital city, one could often saw the scene that two children were standing face-to-face and pulling a rope against with each other to compare who was stronger. Now, during some festivals and group activities, the easy-to-people tug of war is people's one of the most favorite sport games.

Shuttlecock Kicking

Shuttlecock kicking, also known as *Cuanhua* (Clustered Flower) or *Daji* (Cock Hitting), is a type of game to kick shuttlecock with feet or legs. According to historical and archaeological materials,

《高僧传》中记载，南北朝时期的高僧慧光就是一个踢毽子的高手："沙门慧光年方十二，在天街井栏上，反踢蹀，一连五百，众人喧竞，异而观之。"慧光和尚十二岁时在天街井栏（古代水井上的保护架）上反踢（即拐踢）毽子，一次能踢五百下，引得很多人在一旁观看、议论。可见，踢毽子在南北朝时期已经是民间喜闻乐见的游戏项目了。

唐宋时期，踢毽子在民间流传极广，并出现了经营毽子的商铺。

- 《北京民间风俗百图·踢毽子》（清）
One Hundred Paintings of Beijing Folk Customs: Kicking Shuttlecock (Qing Dynasty, 1616-1911)

shuttlecock kicking dates as far back as the Han Dynasty. In 1913, a stone relief carved with eight men playing shuttlecock kicking was unearthed in a tomb of the Eastern Han Dynasty at Zhangcun Village of Yubeitun Town in Jining County, Shandong Province. Shi Daoxuan, a monk of the Tang Dynasty, once recorded in *Biographies of Eminent Monks* that: a 12-years-old monk named Huiguang once played shuttlecock kicking near the guard railing of a well in the Tianjie Street, and he could kick the shuttlecock for 500 times constantly with the technique of reversing kick (i.e. turning kick, *Guaiti*, meaning to kick with the outer ankle), attracting many passersby to watch and discuss his show. So, the shuttlecock has already been a well-received game in the folk since the Southern and Northern dynasties.

During the Tang Dynasty and the Song Dynasty, shuttlecock was widespread in the folk and the shops selling shuttlecock appeared. According to *Origin of Things* written by Gao Cheng in the Song Dynasty (960-1279), children at the time used tin slice as shuttlecock's base, which was inserted with cock feather to make a shuttlecock.

Artists specializing in shuttlecock

● 人们以踢毽子为乐（图片提供：微图）
People Playing Shuttlecock for Fun

宋代高承编撰的《事物纪原》中记载："今时小儿以铅锡为钱，装以鸡羽，呼为毽子，三四成群走踢。"踢毽子是当时小孩子的主要游戏，毽子是在铅锡做成的底座上面插上鸡毛制作而成的。

清代出现了专门从事踢毽子的艺人。清人潘荣陛撰写的杂记《帝京岁时纪胜》中记载："都门有专艺踢毽子者……团转相击，随其高下，动合机宜，不致坠落，亦博戏

kicking appeared in the Qing Dynasty. According to *Jottings of the Capital City* written by Pan Rongbi in the Qing Dynasty, "Near the gate of the city, there are professional shuttlecock artists… they compete with each other in groups by kicking the shuttlecocks nimbly and swiftly to keep them on the air, which can be said to be one of the consummate skills among competing games." Today, shuttlecock kicking prevails widely among the folk, and both adults and children can have fun with it.

中之绝技矣。"如今，踢毽子在民间广泛流行，无论是大人还是儿童都可以以此为乐。

在古代，毽子又称"鞬子"或"跕"，一般是将鸡毛、皮毛、纸条或绒线，插入并固定在外圆内方

In ancient times, shuttlecock was also called *Jianzi* or *Die*, and it was usually made by inserting and fastening cock feathers, furs, paper strips or wools onto a copper-coin base with a round edge and square inside. There are four ways to kick shuttlecock: *Panti* (crossing kick), *Guaiti* (turning kick), *Bengti* (jumping kick) and *Keti* (knocking kick). Crossing kick is to bend a leg, and then kick the shuttlecock inward with inner ankle of another leg; turning kick is to bend a leg, and then kick the shuttlecock outward with outer ankle of another leg; jumping kick is to straighten the leg and foot in a line, and then kick the shuttlecock with foot tip; knocking kick is to bend the leg naturally, and then kick the shuttlecock with thigh or knee. Based on the four types of kicks, more than 100 playing ways have been derived, such as inter-merging kick, which is to use the crossing kick and turning kick in turns. Generally speaking, when children are playing shuttlecock kicking, they may sing songs as well. For example, there

- 沈庆兰《童儿娱毽图》（清）
Painting of Children Kicking Shuttlecock, by Shen Qinglan (Qing Dynasty, 1616-1911)

的铜钱底座中制作而成的。毽子的基本踢法有四种，分别为盘踢、拐踢、蹦踢、磕踢。盘踢是指一腿弯曲，由外侧向内侧摆动，用脚内侧踢毽子。拐踢是指一腿弯曲，由内侧向外侧摆动，用脚踝外侧踢毽子。蹦踢是指将腿、脚绷直成一线，用脚尖踢毽子。磕踢是指腿部自然弯曲，用大腿或膝关节踢毽子。由四种基本踢法衍生出的花样有上百种之多。例如，"里外廉"，是指盘踢、拐踢轮流使用的踢法。一般来讲，儿童踢毽子还会伴随着儿歌一起进行。例如，由清代流传至今的童谣："一个毽儿，踢两半儿，打花鼓，绕花线儿，里踢外拐，八仙过海……"

is a children's song that has been being popular ever since the Qing Dynasty, "A shuttlecock, two and half kick, beat flower drums, wind colored threads, cross inward and turn inward, Eight Immortals crossing the sea…"

- **毽子**（图片提供：微图）
Shuttlecock

> 民俗类游戏

踩高跷

踩高跷，又称"扎高脚""走高腿"，是春节、元宵节的传统习俗之一。

关于踩高跷的起源，有一种说法认为踩高跷源自古代渔民的劳动。在浅海地方，渔民们踩着木棍进行捕鱼作业，以防止身体陷入滩涂中。

早在春秋战国时期，踩高跷就已经出现。战国时期的典籍《列子》中记载了宋国的一个卖艺的人向宋国国君献艺，把比身体长一倍的木棍绑在腿上，一边踩一边耍弄宝剑的情景。高跷在不同时期的名称也有所不同，汉魏时称作"跷技"，宋代时称作"踏桥"，清代

> Folk Games

Stilt Walking

Stilt walking, also called *Zhagaojiao* (High-foot Bundling) or *Zougaotui* (High-leg Walking), is one of the traditional customs during the Spring Festival and Lantern Festival.

As for the origin of stilt walking, there is an explanation believes that stilt walking is derived from ancient fishermen's work. In shallow water areas, fishermen at the time stepped on sticks to conduct fishing, so as to prevent sinking into tidal flats.

As early as in the time from the Spring and Autumn Period to the Warring States Period, stilt walking appeared. The ancient book *Liezi* written during the Warring States Period recorded a scene like this: in the State of Song, an artist had a performance for the king by tying

渔民踩高跷捕鱼（图片提供：FOTOE）
Fishman Walking on Stilts to Conduct Fishing

至今才统称为"高跷"。

现在，踩高跷仍旧是春节、元宵节等传统节日中十分盛行的表演节目，人们在踩高跷的时候往往要装扮成神话传说或历史故事中的人物形象。

高跷为木制，一般以榆木、槐木为最佳。制作高跷时，首先将木

the sticks two times as long as his body to his legs to have a sword dance. Stilt walking has different names in different periods, such as *Qiaoji* (techniques of stilt) during the Han and Wei dynasties, *Taqiao* (stepping bridges) in the Song Dynasty, and *Gaoqiao* which appeared in the Qing Dynasty and spread up to now as the formal name.

Now, stilt walking is still a very popular performance during Spring Festival, Lantern Festival and other traditional festivals when people will walk on stilts and dress up as the characters in mythical legends and historical stories.

As a woodwork, stilts of the best quality are generally made of elm or Chinese scholar tree. To make a stilt, the first thing is to process the wood into a long stick by flatting the upper part and rounding the lower part. And then, the height of the foot pedal should be set up according to the length of the stilt, and

头加工成上扁下圆的长木棍，根据高跷的高度设置脚踏板的高度，脚踏板上有绑腿布绳以固定双腿。按照长度，高跷分为长达两米的高跷和30厘米左右的中跷。按照表演形式的不同，又可分为文跷和武跷。文跷即在踩高跷的过程中边演唱边跳舞，武跷则是踩着高跷表演叠罗汉、倒立、劈叉等高难度动作。

cloth strips should be tied on the foot pedal for leg fastening. In term of length, stilts can be divided into the long ones up to 2 meters and the middle ones of 30 centimeters. In terms of performing forms, stilt walking can be divided into *Wenqiao* (civil stilt) and *Wuqiao* (martial stilt). Civil stilt means to walk on stilts with singing and dancing, and martial stilt contains many difficult actions like human pyramid, headstand, split, etc.

- 正月民俗活动踩高跷（图片提供：FOTOE）
Custom of Stilt Walking During Lunar January

• 天津杨柳青年画《高跷会》（图片提供：FOTOE）
Yangliuqing's New Year Painting in Tianjin: *Meeting of Stilt Walking*

荡秋千

　　荡秋千，是清明节的传统习俗之一，因此清明节又称"秋千节"。唐代欧阳询主编的《艺文类聚》中有"北方山戎，寒食日用秋千为戏"的记载。秋千是由春秋战国时期的北方民族山戎发明的。秋千原名"千秋"，原本只是一根由皮革制成的粗绳子，人们用手抓绳而荡，后来在齐桓公征讨山戎获胜后，"千秋"开始向南流传。

　　汉代时，荡秋千就已十分流行。原有的一根绳子已演变成了

Dang Qiuqian (Swing)

Dang Qiuqian (*Dang* means to swing, and *Qiuqian* means the object of swing) is one of the traditional customs on Pure Brightness Festival, which thus is also called Swing Festival. According to *Collections of Arts and Literatures* compiled by Ouyang Xun in the Tang Dynasty, the Shanrong people in north China once played swing to celebrate the Cold Food Festival. Swing was invented by the Shanrong people in north China at the time from the Spring and Autumn Period to the Warring States Period. Swing was originally called

- 陈枚《月曼清游图册·荡秋千》（清）
  Painting Album of Yueman Qingyou: Swing, by Chen Mei (Qing Dynasty, 1616-1911)

两根绳子加上踏板的形式。唐代高无际作有《汉武帝后庭秋千赋》，其中写道："秋千者，千秋也。汉武祈千秋之寿，故后宫多秋千之乐。"讲述的是汉武帝为了祈求长寿，在宫廷中设秋千来游戏玩乐。为了避讳祝寿的"千秋"一词，千秋被改称为"秋千"。

唐宋时期，荡秋千发展至鼎盛时期。五代时期文学家王仁裕在其笔记《开元天宝遗事》中记载："天宝宫中，至寒食节，竞竖秋千，令宫嫔辈戏笑以为宴乐。帝呼为半仙之戏，都中士民因而呼之。"描述了唐代天宝年间后宫妃嫔荡秋千的情景。古人认为仙人居住在高空，因此唐玄宗称荡秋千的人为"半仙"，荡秋千又称"半仙戏"。唐代诗人王建则在《秋千词》中描述了民间女子荡秋千时的情景："身轻裙薄易生力，双手向空如鸟翼。"宋代时，民间还出现了一种名为"水秋千"的杂技项目，即在船头上架秋千架，人们在秋千上荡至高空，而后翻着跟头跳入水中。

辽金元时期，荡秋千逐渐成为

Qianqiu, which at first was just a thick single leather rope for people to hold and swing. Later, Duke Huan of the State of Qi took on his northern expedition and conquered the Shanrong people, and then the *Qianqiu* began to spread to the south.

In the Han Dynasty, swing had been very popular, and its form had evolved from the original single rope into two ropes with a pedal. According to *Poem of Swing in Imperial Harem of Emperor Wu of the Han Dynasty* written by Gao Wuji in the Tang Dynasty, the name of swing was changed from *Qianqiu* to *Qiuqian* because when Emperor Wu of the Han Dynasty ordered to build lots of swings for playing during his birthday, the word *Qianqiu*, which could be used as a birthday congratulation, was replaced by *Qiuqian* to avoid misunderstandings.

During the Tang Dynastyand the Song Dynasty, the development of swing reached its peak. Wang Renyu, an astronomer of the Five dynasties, once recorded in *Notes on Kaiyuan and Tianbao Periods* that the imperial concubines were fond of swing games in palace during the Tianbao Period (742-756) in the Tang Dynasty. The ancient people believed that the immortals were living in the air, so Emperor Xuanzong

院子里的秋千（图片提供：微图）
The Swing in the Courtyard

男女老少皆宜的日常游戏。元代文人熊梦祥编撰的《析津志》中记载："辽俗最重清明，上自内苑，下至士庶，俱立秋千架，日以嬉戏为乐。"

荡秋千作为清明节的传统习俗保留至今，已经成为人们日常嬉戏娱乐的游戏活动。

of the Tang Dynasty called swing players as Half Immortals and the game of swing was called Game of Half Immortals. Wang Jian, a poet in the Tang Dynasty, once described in *Verse of Swing* the scene of a folk woman playing swing, "Light body and thin skirt are advantages to use strength, and the raising hands look like bird wings." In the Song Dynasty, the folk also appeared an acrobatics called Water Swing, which was to set up a swing on prow, allowing people to swing high and somersault into the water.

During the period of the Liao Dynasty (907-1125), the Jin Dynasty (1115-1234) and the Yuan Dynasty (1206-1368), swing gradually became a daily game suitable for all people regardless of age and sex. According to *Records of Xijin* complied by literate Xiong Mengxiang in the Yuan Dynasty, the custom of Pure Brightness Festival was so important for people of the Liao Dynasty that both the nobility and the multitude would build swings to play for fun.

As a traditional custom of Pure Brightness Festival, the game of swing has been spread up to now, and has become an entertaining activity in people's daily life.

● 小女孩在荡秋千（图片提供：微图）
A Little Girl on a Swing

放风筝

风筝，又叫"风琴""纸鹞""纸鸢"等，起源于中国，被称为"人类最早的飞行器"。西汉刘安撰写的《淮南子》中有关于春秋战国时期木鸢的记载，清代文学家曹雪芹认为这是传统风筝的雏形。

东汉时期，蔡伦发明造纸术，推动了木鸢向纸鸢的发展。南北朝时期，纸风筝出现。北宋文学家司马光编撰的《资治通鉴》中记载："有羊车儿献策作鸱（即纸鸢），

Kite Flying

Kite, also known as *Fengqin*, *Zhiyao* (paper snipe), *Zhiyuan* (paper eagle), etc., originated in China and was praised as "the earliest human spacecraft". In *Huainanzi*, which was written by Liu'an in the Western Han Dynasty, there was a record about the wooden eagle of the time from the Spring and Autumn Period to the Warring States Period, which was regarded as the rudiment of traditional kites by Cao Xueqin in the Qing Dynasty.

In the Eastern Han Dynasty (25-

• 徐渭所画儿童放风筝图（明）
Painting of Children Flying Kites, by Xu Wei (Ming Dynasty, 1368-1644)

系以长绳，写敕于内，放以从风，冀达众军。"讲述的是公元549年，南朝梁武帝的臣子侯景叛乱，将梁武帝困于京都建康（今江苏南京）的台城宫殿中，有人向梁武帝建议将载有武帝求援诏令的纸鸢放飞以通知援军前来营救。

"风筝"一词，最早出现在五代时期。人们在原有的纸鸢上安装竹笛，使之在风中飞行时能够发出类似古筝的声响，故名"风筝"。

220), Cai Lun's invention of papermaking promoted the evolvement of wooden eagle into paper eagle. By the Southern and Northern dynasties, the paper kite emerged. Sima Guang, a litterateur of the Northern Song Dynasty, once recorded in his *History as a Mirror* that: in 549, under the reign of Emperor Wu of Liang during the Southern dynasties, the courtier Hou Jing rose in rebellion and trapped the emperor in the Taicheng Palace in the capital city Jiankang (current

唐宋时期，放风筝已十分盛行，且制作工艺有了很大发展，出现了丝绢扎制的风筝。据史料记载，公元713年，唐玄宗李隆基曾在山东蓬莱观看名为"八仙过海"的风筝放飞。宋代时出现了专门制作风筝的手工艺人和专门出售风筝的店铺，以及被称作"赶趁人"的专门从事放风筝表演的艺人。宋徽宗就是一个风筝爱好者，他主持编撰了中国最早的一部风筝专著《宣和风筝谱》，记述了有关风筝的绑扎、绘制技术及材料的选用等方面的内容。

明清时期，风筝常常出现在文学、绘画等作品中。明代著名画家

- 蜻蜓形风筝
  Dragonfly-shaped Kite

Nanjing City, Jiangsu Province), and at this time, the emperor was suggested to write down the order of rescue on paper eagles, which were flight to inform the reinforcements.

The Chinese word *Fengzheng* (kite) first appeared in the Five dynasties. People installed bamboo flute onto the paper eagle, to make it sounded like a kind of plucked instrument named *Guzheng* in the wind, so paper eagle was then called *Fengzheng* (*Feng* means wind in Chinese).

During the Tang Dynasty and the Song Dynasty, kite flying had been very popular and its production process had made significant progress that the silk-made kites appeared. According to historical records, Li Longji (Emperor Xuanzong of the Tang Dynasty), went to Penglai of Shandong Province in 713 to watch the flying of the kite named Eight Immortals Crossing the Sea. By the Song Dynasty, there had been craftsmen specializing in kite making, shops selling kites and artists living on kite flying. The big kite fan Emperor Huizong hosted the compilation of China's earliest kite monograph *Genealogy of Kites During Xuanhe Period*, recording the colligating and drawing techniques, the selection of

徐渭十分喜欢放风筝,曾创作了25幅《风鸢图诗》,其中有一幅画中写道:"江北江南低鹞齐,线长线短回高低。"曹雪芹对风筝颇有研究,曾经撰写过一本名为《南鹞北鸢考工志》的风筝专著。在其文学著作《红楼梦》中,有一首关于风筝的诗:"阶下儿童仰面时,清明妆点最堪宜。游丝一断浑无力,莫向东风怨别离。"

清末诗人高鼎有一首诗作《村居》,描写了春天时儿童趁着东风放风筝的情景:"草长莺飞二月天,拂堤杨柳醉春烟。儿童散学归

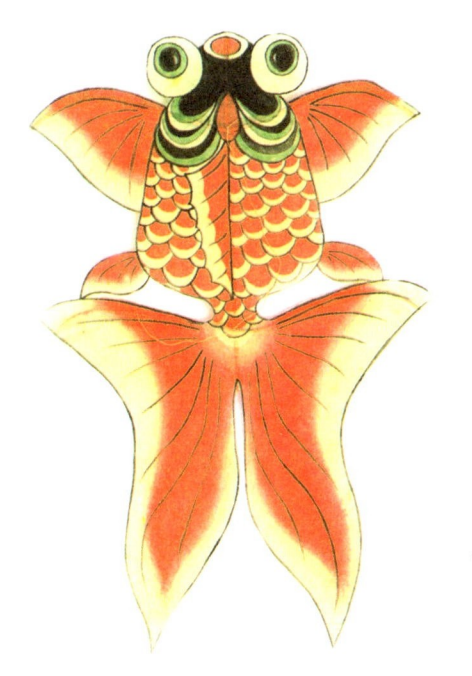

materials and other aspects of kite.

During the Ming Dynasty and the Qing Dynasty, kite often appeared in literary works, paintings, and so on. Xu Wei, a famous painter in the Ming Dynasty, was so keen on kite flying that he created 25 *Kite Paintings with Poems*, one of which says, "Kites are flying in the northern and southern sides of the river, the lines are wound up or paid off to control the kite in the sky." With an intensive study on kites, Cao Xueqin wrote a kite monograph called *Study Notes of Kites in North and South*. In his novel *Dream of Red Mansion*, Cao Xueqin wrote a poem about kite, "In spring boys look up to the sky and stare it, on Pure Brightness Festival it appears everywhere. The strength all goes when once the bond is parted, and on the wind it drifts off broken-hearted."

Gao Ding, a poet in the late Qing Dynasty, wrote a poem named *Village Life*, which describes a scene that children flew kites by the eastern wind

• 鱼形风筝
Fish-shaped Kite

• 《北京民间风俗百图·放风筝》（清）
One Hundred Paintings of Beijing Folk Customs: Kite Flying (Qing Dynasty, 1616-1911)

in lunar February, a time when grasses sprouted out, nightingales flew into the sky, and willows swung in the gentle breeze and spring smoke. Today, such kite-flying scenes during the spring are very common. Since 1984, the International Kite Festival has been held almost every year in Weifang City (Shandong Province), which is known as the hometown of kite, attracting kite lovers from all over the world.

Kite-making can be divided into three steps: framework building, paper pasting and pattern drawing. The first step is to use bamboo to build kite frameworks in shapes like butterfly and eagle. The second step is to paste paper, silk and other materials on the framework. The third step is to draw on a variety of patterns, most of which are generally auspicious patterns.

来早，忙趁东风放纸鸢。"如今，这种春日放风筝的景象已十分普遍。自1984年起，被誉为"风筝故乡"的山东潍坊基本上每年都要举办国际风筝节，来自世界各地的风筝爱好者在此欢聚一堂。

制作风筝可分为扎、糊、绘三个部分，即扎架子、糊纸面、绘花彩。首先，要用竹子扎制成风筝的骨架，例如蝴蝶形、老鹰形等，然后在竹骨架上糊上纸张或丝绢等材

● 小女孩在放风筝（图片提供：微图）
A Little Girl Is Flying a Kite

料，并绘制上各种图案，一般以具有吉祥寓意的图案居多。

赛龙舟

赛龙舟又称"龙舟竞渡""龙船赛会"。自古以来，龙被视作中华民族的图腾。在赛龙舟活动中，人们都要将船只雕刻成龙形或绘有龙的图案，故名"龙舟"。

早在原始社会时期，长江中下游地区就有赛龙舟的传统。赛龙舟

Loong Boat Racing

Loong boat racing is called *Longzhou Jingdu* or *Longzhou Saihui* in Chinese. Since ancient times, loong has been regarded as the totem of the Chinese nation. During the activities of loong boat racing, people will carve boats in the shape of loong or paint them with loong patterns, so they are called Loong Boat.

As early as in primitive society, there was a tradition of loong boat racing among the people living in the middle

必须依赖河流才能进行，因此活动范围主要集中在多水的中国南方地区。赛龙舟也是端午节的传统习俗之一。据传，端午节赛龙舟起源于战国时期纪念诗人屈原的活动。

唐宋时期，赛龙舟发展至鼎盛时期，《旧唐书》中有唐穆宗"观竞渡"的记载。唐代诗人张建封在《竞渡歌》中写道："鼓声三下红旗开，两龙跃出浮水来。棹影斡波飞万剑，鼓声劈浪鸣千雷。鼓声渐急标将近，两龙望标目如瞬。坡上人呼霹雳惊，竿头彩挂虹蜺晕。前船抢水已得标，后船失势空挥桡。"从诗作中可以看出当时赛龙舟的规则：龙舟比赛在鼓声中进行，当龙舟临近终点时，会有人从标船（停泊在终点的船只）上将系有红锦缎的活鸭子、活鹅等放入水中，称之为"锦标"。在划到终点时，龙舟上的水手需跳入水中夺得锦标才算胜出。

明代时，都城北京也已经出现了赛龙舟活动。明代刘若愚撰写的《明宫史》中记载了万历皇帝每年端午节都要到皇家园林西苑赛龙舟的史实。清代宫廷延续了明代的传

and lower reaches of the Yangtze River. As it must be held on rivers, the activity of loong boat racing mainly takes place in southern China with lots of rivers. Loong boat racing is also a traditional custom of Loong Boat Festival (Duanwu Festival). Allegedly, this custom originated in the activities of memorizing the poet Qu Yuan of the Warring States Period.

During the Tang Dynasty and Song Dynasty, loong boat racing came to its heyday, and there was a record that Emperor Muzong of the Tang Dynasty went to "watch the boat racing". The *Song of Boat Racing* written by Zhang Jianfeng in the Tang Dynasty recorded, "After three beats of the drum, behind the red flags, two loong boats appears. The boats run through the waves to the rhythm of the drum. While the drum beat gets faster, the finish line is in our sight. With the hail of the audience and flying colorful banners, the first boat crosses the finish line while the second one is out of control." We can find out the rules of loong boat racing at the time: it took place with the sound of drums, and when the loong boat reached the finishing line, live ducks or geese tied with red brocades, which were regarded as the prize for winners, called *Jinbiao*,

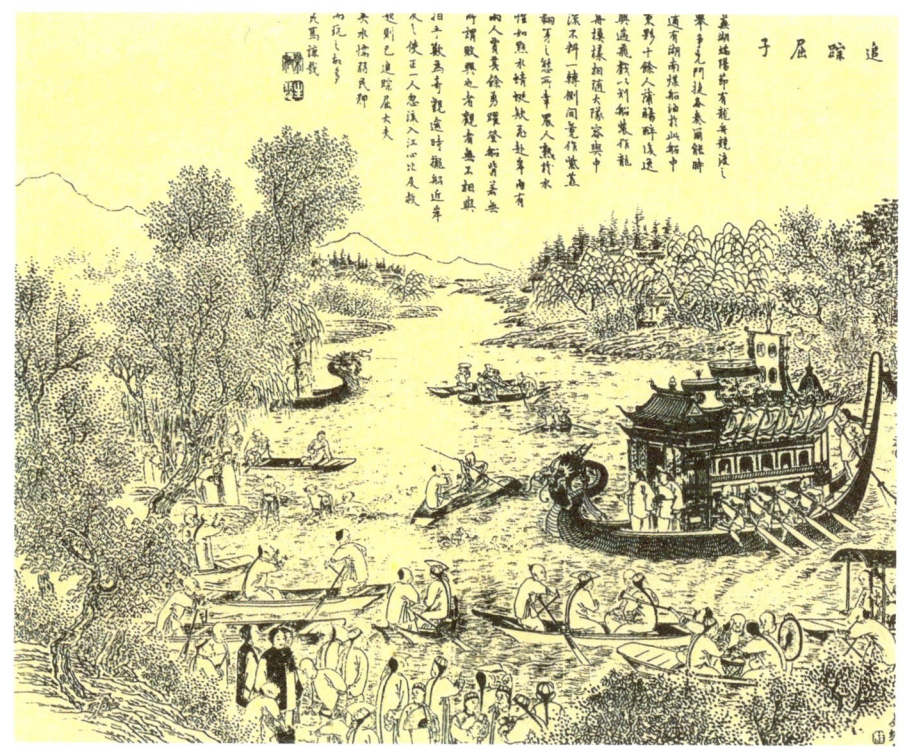

《追踪屈子》（出自《点石斋画报》）（图片提供：FOTOE）
《追踪屈子》表现的是安徽芜湖地区以赛龙舟的形式吊唁屈原的民俗活动。

Tracing Qu Yuan, from *Pictorial of Dian Shi Zhai*
Tracing Qu Yuan is a traditional custom of memorizing Qu Yuan during the loong boat racing held in Wuhu City of Anhui Province.

统，每年端午节也要在西苑举行赛龙舟比赛。而在民间，赛龙舟也十分流行，《帝京岁时纪胜》中有相关记载："前临运河，五月朔至端阳日，于河内斗龙舟，夺锦标，香会纷纭，游人络绎。"

would be released into the water from the marking boat (the boat mooring at the finishing line); at this time, the boating men who had reach the finishing line and jumped into the water to catch the *Jinbiao* (ducks and geese) won the game.

In the Ming Dynasty, loong boat racing appeared in Beijing. According to

History of Ming Palace written by Liu Ruoyu in the Ming Dynasty, Emperor Wanli went to the royal garden of Xiyuan to participate in loong boat racing on every year's Loong Boat Festival. Inheriting this tradition, in the royal garden of the Qing Dynasty, emperors also held loong boat racing at every year's Loong Boat Festival. Meanwhile, loong boat racing was also very popular in the folk. According to *Jottings of the Capital City*, loong boat racings were held on the canal during the time from lunar May 1st to 5th, and all people of the whole city would go out to watch the games.

- 《五月竞舟》（清）

  出自《清院画十二月令图》，描绘了清代宫廷在五月赛龙舟的场景。《月令图》是中国传统风俗画。此图册共十二张，以圆明园为蓝本，描绘了宫廷在十二个月中的生活场景。

  Loong Boat Racing in Lunar May (Qing Dynasty, 1616-1911)

  Excerpted from *Paintings of Qing Palace in Twelve Lunar Months*, this painting depicts the scene of loong boat racing held in the palace of the Qing Dynasty in Lunar May. As a kind of Chinese traditional genre painting, the album of *Paintings of Qing Palace in Twelve Lunar Months* contains 12 such paintings, modeling the Summer Palace to depict the lives in palace during twelve lunar months.

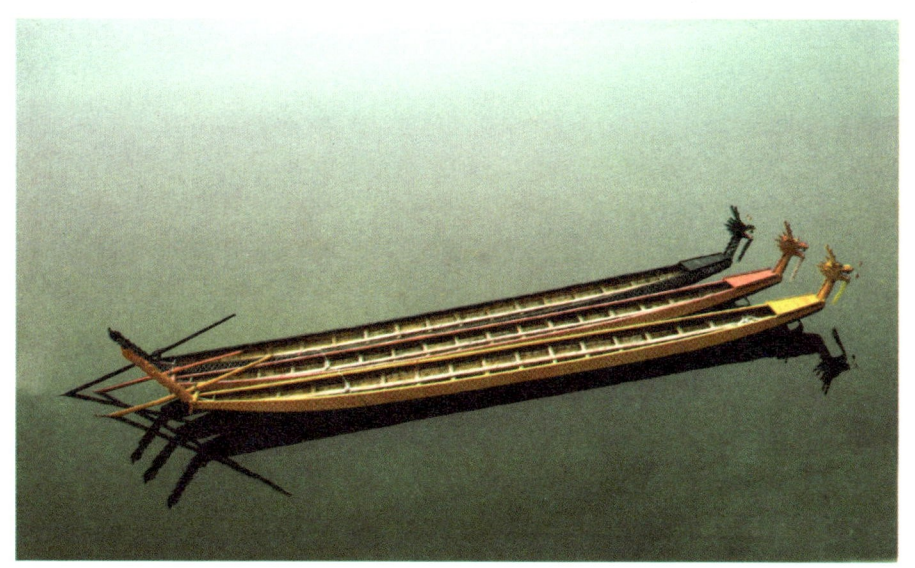

- 停在水上的龙舟（图片提供：FOTOE）
  Loong Boats on the Water

- 龙舟比赛
  Loong Boat Racing

• 端阳龙舟（出自明代《唐诗画谱》）
Loong Boat Racing on Loong Boat Festival (from *Paintings of Tang Poems* written in the Ming Dynasty, 1368-1644)

乞巧

《荆楚岁时记》中记载："七月七日为牵牛织女聚会之夜……是夕，人家妇女结彩缕，穿七孔针，或以金银鍮石为针，陈几筵、酒脯、瓜果于庭中以乞巧，有喜子网于瓜上则以为符应。"在古代，女子必须掌握刺绣、纺织、缝纫等

- 《六夕乞巧》（出自《点石斋画报》）

（图片提供：FOTOE）

Talent Praying at Night of Lunar July 6th (from Pictorial of Dianshi Zhai)

Talent Praying

According to *Festivals and Traditions of Jingchu People*, "Lunar July 7th was the night for Cowherd and Weaver…Women at the night would have talent praying by waving festoons, threading 7 needles or whetting gold or silk into needles; and if there was a spider to weave a net on the melons or fruits placed in the hall, they would be regarded as talented weavers." In ancient times, the women had to be capable of embroidery, weaving, sewing and other needle works. Therefore, on lunar July 7th, women needed to take needle works, and if there were spiders to weave nets on the melons or fruits, it would be a successful talent praying. That's why Double Seventh Festival was also called Talent Praying Festival.

As early as in the Han Dynasty, talent praying had appeared. At that time, women would put a little red spider in caskets or other containers, allowing it to weave a net, and then would open the container to see the density of the net the next day, so as to judge whether the women were talented. Meanwhile, talent praying could be conducted by threading: women competed to thread needles in the moonlight, and those who could thread 7

女红（gōng）。因此在七夕节这一天，女子们不但要穿针引线，还要看是否有蜘蛛在瓜果上结网，如有则被视为乞巧应验的标志。因此七夕节又称"乞巧节"。

早在汉代时，乞巧就已经出现。当时，女子们将红色的小蜘蛛放在首饰盒等器物中让其结网，等到第二天打开，观察织网的疏密来判断女子的巧拙。同时还有穿针乞巧的方式：女子们在月光下比赛穿针，看谁能够将七根彩线分别穿过七个针孔，以速度的快慢判断巧拙。

唐宋时期，每年七夕节家家户户都要为女子进行乞巧。唐代诗人林杰的诗作《乞巧》就还原了当时的情景："七夕今宵看碧霄，牵牛织女渡河桥。家家乞巧望秋月，穿尽红丝几万条。"当时在宫廷中也有乞巧活动，《开元天宝遗事》中记载了唐玄宗时期在宫中举办乞巧仪式的情景：宫人在宫中悬挂精美的织锦，陈列瓜果、酒肉祭祀牛郎和织女，嫔妃们则拿着九孔针、五色线等对着月亮穿针引线。

明清两代，乞巧仍旧十分流行，

color lines across 7 pinholes fastest would be the winner.

During the period of the Tang Dynasty and the Song Dynasty, all families would have talent praying for women on every year's Double Seventh Festival. Such a scene was represented in the poem Talent Praying written by poet Lin Jie of the Tang Dynasty, "Look up to the clear sky at the night of Double Seventh Festival, Cowherd (Altair) and Weaver (Vega) are crossing the Milky Way by bridge. All families are having talent praying in the autumn moonlight, threading tens of thousands of red silks." At that time, the activities of talent praying also took place in the palace. *Notes on Kaiyuan and Tianbao Periods* once recorded the ceremony of talent praying in palace during the reign of Emperor Xuanzong of the Tang Dynasty: with elegant brocades hung in the palace, melons and fruits were placed to worship Cowherd and Weaver, and concubines are using nine-hole needles or five-color lines to thread under the moon.

During the Ming Dynasty and the Qing Dynasty, talent praying was still of great popularity, and the way of throwing needles for talent praying appeared at the time. Specifically, this way was to place a

- 《七月乞巧》（清）

出自《清院画十二月令图》。画中描绘了乞巧节当天，妃嫔、宫女设乞巧宴、许愿的场景。

Talent Praying in Lunar July (Qing Dynasty, 1616-1911)

Excerpted from *Paintings of Qing Palace in Twelve Lunar Months*, this painting depicts the scene of concubines and maids' banqueting and wishing during talent praying on Talent Praying Festival.

出现了投针乞巧的方式。具体方法是在七夕节前一天，将盛有一半井水和一半雨水的碗露天放置，第二天再放到太阳下暴晒，中午时将绣花针投入水中，来观看针在水中的影子。明代刘侗撰写的《帝京景物略》中对此有详细记载："有成云物、花头、鸟兽影者，有成鞋及剪刀、水茄影者，谓乞得巧。其影粗如锤、细如丝、直如轴蜡，此拙征矣。"意思是说如果针影呈花鸟走兽、鞋或剪刀等形状的，

bowl containing half well water and half rainwater in the open on the day before Double Seventh Festival, expose the bowl to the sun the next day, and then throw an embroidery needle into the water at noon, so as to observe its shadow in the water. According to *Summary of Sceneries in the Capital City* written by Liu Dong in the Ming Dynasty, if the shadow of the needle had a shape like flower, bird, beast, shoe or scissor, it would be a successful talent praying; if the shadow of the needle had a shape like hammer or hair, it would be a symbol of clumsiness. In addition, there was another way of throwing bean sprouts for talent praying: at the night of every lunar year's July 7th, woman threw a previously-soaked bean sprout into a pot, so as to observe the shadow on the bottom of the pot. If the shadow looked like a spinning wheel, loom or flower, it would signify that the woman was

就说明乞巧得应；如果影子像锤子、发丝，则是手拙的象征。除此之外，还有投巧芽（即豆芽）的方式：每年七月初七晚上，女子们将事先泡好的豌豆芽投入盆中，观看盆底的影子，如果像纺车、织布机或花朵，则意味着会纺织，可能是个刺绣能手；如果影子像菜刀、水瓢、锅碗等，则意味着会煮饭、炒菜，可能是个煮饭能手；如果影子像凤冠霞帔，则意味着将来可能会出人头地、大富大贵，可能做官宦夫人。

capable of spinning and might become a skillful spinner; if the shadow looked like a kitchen knife, bailer, pan, bowl, etc., it would signify that the woman was capable of cooking and might become an excellent cook; and if the shadow looked like a phoenix coronet or official robe, it would signify that the women had a bright future of wealth and might become a wife of government official.

> 风雅类游戏

曲水流觞

　　曲水流觞，源自名为"袚禊"（又称"修禊"）的古老祭祀仪式，最初是上巳节的传统习俗，后逐渐成为文人们的风雅游戏。

> Elegant Games

Drifting Wine Cups Along Winding Water

The game of drifting wine cups along winding water originated from the old sacrificial ceremony of *Fuxi*, also known as *Xiuxi* (*Fu* refers to a ceremony aimed to eradicate disasters and pray for blesses

- 仇英《兰亭图》扇面（明）
  Folding Fan's Painting: *Orchid Pavilion*, by Qiu Ying (Ming Dynasty, 1368-1644)

• 陶觞（东汉）

觞是古代的一种酒器，有木制、陶制和玉制等。陶制酒觞，有双耳，又称"羽觞"，体积较大，可放于荷叶上，使其顺流而下。

Clay Wine Cup (Eastern Han Dynasty, 25-220)

It is a kind of drinking vessel in ancient China, which can be made of wood, clay jade, etc. The clay wine cup has two ears, also called feather wine cup (*Yushang*, *Yu* means feathers in Chinese). It is of heavy weight and can be placed on the lotus leaves and drift downward.

上巳节，又称"女儿节"，"上巳"一词最早出现在《后汉书》中。古时，上巳节为每年农历三月上旬的第一个巳日，故名。魏晋以后，上巳节改为三月初三。从春秋战国时期开始，每年的上巳节，人们为了除去身上的疾病、灾祸或不祥，都要到水边举行祭祀仪式，包括采兰、沐浴等，仪式之后往往还有嬉游、曲水流觞等活动。

in ancient China, and *Xi* means a sacrifice held by river in spring and summer in hope of removing the inauspicious in ancient China). At first it was a traditional custom in the Shangsi Festival and later gradually became an elegant game popular among literati.

The Chinese word *Shangsi* appeared in *History of the Han Dynasty* for the first time, and Shangsi Festival, also known as Girl's Day, got this name because it falls on the first *Si* (the sixth of the twelve Earthly Branches) Day in the first ten-day period of the annual lunar March. After the Wei Dynasty (220-265) and the Jin Dynasty (265-420), Shangsi Festival was fixed on lunar March 3rd. From the Spring and Autumn Period and the Warring States Period, people would conduct sacrificial ceremonies, including picking orchids and taking a shower by river side during the festival so as to get rid of illnesses, calamities and misfortunes. Afterwards, there were other activities going on, such as water games and drifting wine cups along winding water.

The game of drifting wine cups along winding water indicates a recreational activity in which people sit along the winding river banks, place wine

曲水流觞是指人们坐于弯曲流淌的河渠两岸，将酒觞（即酒杯）放于上游水面上，让其顺流而下，酒觞停在谁的面前谁就要拿起饮酒。曲水流觞的形式主要有三种：第一种是自然河水的流觞；第二种是凿石成曲水的流觞，例如各种流杯亭中的曲水；第三种就是宴会酒桌上的流觞。

汉代时，已有"引流饮觞、递成曲水"的说法。自汉代至唐代，曲水流觞不仅要饮酒，参加者还要赋诗。

魏晋南北朝时期至唐代，曲水

cups in the upper water and drift them downstream. When the cup stops floating, the one nearest to it must pick it up and drink the wine. There are three major ways to play the game, namely drifting along natural rivers, drifting along man-made stone channel (like varieties of drifting pavilions), and drifting along the banquet table.

In the Han Dynasty, there was a saying as "drifting wine cups along winding water". Then in the Tang Dynasty, aside from drinking, participants were required to improvise poems.

From the period of the Wei, Jin, and Southern and Northern dynasties to

- 文徵明《兰亭修禊图》（明）

Exorcism by Orchid Pavilion, by Wen Zhengming (Ming Dynasty, 1368-1644)

- **冯承素摹《兰亭集序》（唐）**

  王羲之，东晋书法家，被后世尊称为"书圣"，王羲之的《兰亭集序》被誉为"天下第一行书"。

  Preface of Orchid Pavilion Collection, Copied by Feng Chengsu (Tang Dynasty, 618-907)

  Wang Xizhi, a calligrapher in the Eastern Jin Dynasty, is honored by later generations as Saint of Calligraphy with his masterpieces hailed as the Best Running Script in China.

流觞备受文人、士大夫的推崇。《荆楚岁时记》中记载："三月三日，士民并出江渚池沼间，为流杯曲水之饮。"公元353年，书法家王羲之和其子王献之、王凝之及辞赋家、高僧等四十一位名士，在会稽（今浙江绍兴）山阴的兰亭举行集会。在祓禊之后，四十一位名士依次坐在溪水的两岸，饮酒赋诗。王羲之的《兰亭集序》讲述了兰亭的美景和集会上的盛况。这是有关曲水流觞的有名的历史记载。公元683年，唐代诗人王勃也与友人举行了一场曲水流觞活动，并仿照王羲之

the Tang Dynasty, this game was highly praised by literati and officialdom. According to *Festivals and Traditions of Jingchu People*, on lunar March 3rd, literati and common people all went to the riverside to play the game of drifting wine cups along winding water. In 353, forty-one celebrities including calligrapher Wang Xizhi, his two sons Wang Xianzhi and Wang Ningzhi as well as several poets and eminent monks held a rally in Orchid Pavilion in Shanyin County, Kuaiji City (today's Shaoxing City of Zhejiang Province). After an exorcism, the forty-one celebrities began to drink and write poems, sitting in due

的《兰亭集序》创作了一篇《修禊云门献之山亭序》。

宋元明清时期，曲水流觞之风逐渐衰微。

order along the stream banks. The famous *Preface of Orchid Pavilion Collection* by Wang Xizhi describes the beautiful scenery around Orchid Pavilion and the spectacle of this event which is a famous historical record of drifting wine cups along winding water. In 683, Wang Bo, a poet of the Tang Dynasty (618-907) played this game with his friends. Like Wang Xizhi, he also wrote *Preface to the Poem Collection Written in Wang Xianzhi's Pavilion near Yunmen Temple*.

From the Song Dynasty to the Qing Dynasty, drifting wine cups along winding water has been on the wane.

- 北京恭王府流杯亭
Drifting Pavilion in Prince Gong's Mansion in Beijing

茗战

茗战，又称"斗茶""斗茗"，是古人品评茶叶优劣的一种比赛。茶是中国的传统饮品，中国的茶文化具有十分悠久的历史，唐代陆羽在《茶经》中写道："茶之为饮，发乎神农氏，闻于鲁周公。"上古时代的神农氏最早发现了茶，而西周时期鲁国的周公旦则是第一位弘扬茶文化的人。

茗战，早在唐代就已出现，源于贡茶制度，最早出现在盛产贡茶的福建茶乡。每年清明节前后，人们都要举办盛大的茶宴，请名士前

Tea Competition

Tea competition, also known as tea fighting, is a contest to taste and judge tea in ancient China. Tea is a traditional beverage in China and China enjoys a very long history of tea culture. Lu Yu of the Tang Dynasty wrote in *The Classic of Tea*, "Tea drinking dates back to the period of Shennong (ancient Chinese god of agriculture) and becomes famous during the period of the Duke of Lu in the Zhou Dynasty." In ancient times, Shennong discovered tea for the first time, and Dan, Duke of Lu in the Western Zhou Dynasty is the first to develop the tea culture.

- 《清明茶宴图》（唐）
Painting of a Tea Banquet on Pure Brightness Festival (Tang Dynasty, 618-907)

• 古代斗茶图
The Ancient Tea Competition

来品尝和审定贡茶的质量。宋代时，茗战又称"斗茶"。由于此时将唐代的煮茶（指将茶叶碾碎后直接放入茶釜中烹煮）改为点茶，使得茗战发展至鼎盛时期。点茶就是将碾成粉末的茶叶用"不老不嫩"的开水冲点，用竹制的调茶工具茶筅"击拂"（即搅拌），使茶末与

Having emerged early in the Tang Dynasty, the tea competition originated from the tradition of tea tribute and took place for the first time in a homeland of the tribute tea in Fujian Province. Every year around the time of Pure Brightness Festival, people would hold grand tea parties and invite celebrities to taste and judge tea as tribute. In the Song Dynasty,

● 刘松年《斗茶图》（南宋）
Painting of a Tea Fighting in a Tea Garden, by Liu Songnian (Southern Song Dynasty, 1127-1279)

the tea competition was called tea fight instead, and the heyday of tea competition also came, because at that time, grinded tea began to replace boiling tea in the Tang Dynasty. Brewing the grinded tea was conducted in this way: grind tea leaves into powder and boil them in water at an appropriate temperature, neither hot nor cold. Then keep stirring with a tea whisk (a kind of bamboo tool for making tea) until the powder is fully mixed with water. Then the guest can enjoy the hot tea. The tea fight was not only popular among the common people but also in the courtyard during the Song Dynasty. Emperor Huizong of the Song Dynasty once even wrote *Treatise on Tea*, in which the fashion of tea fight was recorded in details.

Nowadays, Chinese tea culture prevails across the world. As an important part of it, the tea fight has attracted wide attention. Many tea lovers are engaged in this activity.

Fresh tea leaves and living water

沸水充分融合，并趁热饮用。斗茶在宋代宫廷中也极为盛行。宋徽宗曾亲自撰写《大观茶论》，其中就详细记载了当时的斗茶之风。

如今，中国茶文化风靡世界，斗茶作为其重要的组成部分，受到了广泛的关注，在民间有众多的茶文化爱好者参与其中。

茗战讲究茶"新"、水"活"：茶叶以清明节前后的嫩茶为佳，点茶时的沸水要"不老不嫩"。判断茗战胜负的标准有两点：一是汤色，二是汤花。汤色是指茶水的颜色。古人有"斗茶先斗色"的说法，观察茶水的颜色就可以知道茶叶的质量和蒸茶的火候。汤色呈纯白色，说明茶质鲜嫩，蒸茶的火候也适宜；汤色呈青白色，说明蒸茶的火候不够；汤色呈灰白色，说明蒸茶的火候大了；汤色呈黄白色，说明茶质过老。

are the two most important things for tea competition: tender tea picked around the time of Pure Brightness Festival tends to be the best and the boiling water for grinded tea should be at a perfectly appropriate temperature, neither hot nor cold. There are two criteria for a winner in a tea fight: first, tea color, and second, tea foam. As the ancient saying goes color is the most important judgment criterion in a tea fight, the color of tea can tell the quality of tea leaves and the timing of tea boiling. For example, tea that appears pure white indicates the tea

- **兔毫盏（南宋）**

因其黑色釉面上的筋脉犹如兔毛，故名。为了衬托汤色之白，宋人以青、墨色的瓷器为上品，其中以兔毫盏为最佳。

Porcelain Wine Cup with Rabbit Hair Glaze (Southern Song Dynasty, 1127-1279)

The rabbit hair glaze gets its name because the veins on the black glaze are just like rabbit hair. In order to set off the whiteness of tea through contrast, people regarded cyan and ink porcelain as high-end tea containers for tea judgment in the Song Dynasty, of which wine cup with rabbit hair glaze ranked the best of all.

汤花是指茶水表面泛起的泡沫，古时称作"沫饽"。在冲泡茶叶时，先将适量磨成粉末的茶叶用沸水调和成膏状，再添加沸水冲泡，边添边用茶匙击拂，使茶汤表面出现汤花，汤花多且持续时间长的胜出。

斗草

斗草，又称"斗百草"，百草即各种花草，具有不同的药性，这源自古代端午节采百草的习俗。《事物纪原》中记载："竞采百药，谓百草以蠲除毒气，故世有斗草之戏。"农历五月天气炎热、疾病多发，因此每年的五月初五端午节，人们都要采集百草以防御疾病。

"斗草"一词最早出现在汉代，西汉申培在《诗说》中写道："《苤苢》，童儿斗草嬉戏歌谣之词赋也。"申培认为中国最早的一部诗歌总集《诗经》中的《苤苢》篇是西周时期儿童斗草时所唱的歌谣。由此可见，自西周至汉代，斗草游戏十分普遍。

南北朝时期，端午节斗草已成为民间十分流行的游戏。《荆楚岁

leaves are fresh and delicate, and the heat control is appropriate; bluish white indicates undercooked; hoary indicates overcooked; yellowish-white indicates the tea leaves are too old; etc.

Tea foam refers to the foam on the surface of tea, known as *Mobo* in ancient times. When making tea, firstly mix grinded tea powders with boiling water into a paste. While adding boiling water, keep stirring the tea with tea spoon until the foam comes out on the surface of tea. The amount and the duration of the foam can help identify the winner.

Grass Stem Fight

Grass stem fight is also known as *Dou Baicao* (Hundred Grass Fight). In Chinese, it means fighting with a hundred varieties of grass stems, namely various plants of different medical properties. It originates from the custom of gathering herbs at the Loong Boat Festival. It is recorded in *Origin of Things* that people rushed to gather herbs in the hope of eradicating poisonous things and the grass stem fight thus came into being. Since the weather is hot and diseases tend to spread quickly in lunar May, people would gather various herbs to prevent diseases.

• 陈洪绶《斗草图》（明）
Painting of Grass Stem Fight, by Chen Hongshou (Ming Dynasty, 1368-1644)

The Chinese words of grass stem fight (*Doucao*) first appeared in the Han Dynasty. Shen Pei of the Western Han Dynasty wrote a ballad sung by children while playing grass stem fight called *Fuyi* (a kind of plant) collected in his book *About Poems*. He also thought the poem *Fuyi* collected in the *Book of Songs* was the ballad sung by children when they were playing this game in the Western Zhou Dynasty (1046 B.C.-771 B.C.). Therefore, from the Western Zhou Dynasty to the Han Dynasty, this game has been widespread.

During the period of the Southern and Northern dynasties, grass stem fight became a very popular game among the common people at the Loong Boat Festival. It is recorded in *Festivals and Traditions of Jingchu People* that "on lunar May 5th, people from all walks of life step on plants for grass stem fight", which means on that day, all the folks went out to gather various herbs and play that game.

During the period of the Tang Dynasty and the Song Dynasty, this game was popular among women and children, and often appeared in literary works. Bai Juyi, a poet of the Tang Dynasty once wrote in his poem *Watching Children*

• 金廷标《群婴斗草图轴》（清）

清代画家金廷标所绘，上有乾隆皇帝题诗。此图描绘了当时儿童嬉戏斗草的场景。

Children Playing Grass Stem Fight, by Jin Tingbiao (Qing Dynasty, 1616-1911)

It is drawn by Jin Tingbiao, a painter of the Qing Dynasty, on which Emperor Qianlong inscribed a poem. The picture describes children's playing grass stem fight at that time.

时记》中记载："五月五日，四民并蹋百草，又有斗百草之戏。"意思是说端午节时，所有的百姓都外出采百草、斗百草。

唐宋时期，斗草深受女子、儿童的喜爱，且常常出现在文学作品中。唐代诗人白居易在《观儿戏》中写道："弄尘复斗草，尽日乐嬉嬉。"唐代诗人崔颢在诗作《王家少妇》中描述了嫁入王家的女子斗百草而忘记梳妆的情景："闲来斗

Playing Games, "Playing grass stem fight in the floating dust, children have funs all day long so cheerfully." In the poem *Young Women from the Wangs*, Cui Hao, another poet of the Tang Dynasty wrote, "Young women spend free time on grass stem fight, so enjoyable that they even forget to put on the make-up." At that time, besides in spare time, people also made varieties of bets on the grass stem fight to increase challenge. In the poem *Gathering Mulberry Leaves*, by Zheng

百草，度日不成妆。"当时，人们不仅在闲暇时以斗草取乐，还常常押上各种赌注以增加挑战，唐代郑谷的诗作《采桑》就有"何如斗百草，赌取凤凰钗"之句。宋代斗草之风比唐代更甚，北宋文学家苏轼描写了人们为了斗草，在深林中搜集花草的场景："寻芒空茂林，斗草得幽兰。"南宋女词人李清照在词作《浣溪沙》中也有关于斗草的描述："海燕未来人斗草，江梅已过柳

Gu, a poet in the Tang Dynasty, it says, "How about making a bet of a phoenix hairpin on a grass stem fight?" This game underwent a larger popularity in the Song Dynasty even than the Tang Dynasty. Literati of the Northern Song Dynasty, Su Shi once depicted people's searching for grass stem deep in the forest for playing the game, "Search for awn in the vast thick forest, and obtain orchid for the game at last." In the verse *Silk-Washing Stream,* a female poet Li Qingzhao of the Southern Song Dynasty described the scene of grass stem fight, "Petrels have not yet come and people are playing grass stem fight; plums have already matured and fluffy catkins from blooming willows are flying in the air; after a light rain at dusk, the swing becomes wet." Even until the Ming Dynasty and the Qing Dynasty, this game still prevailed.

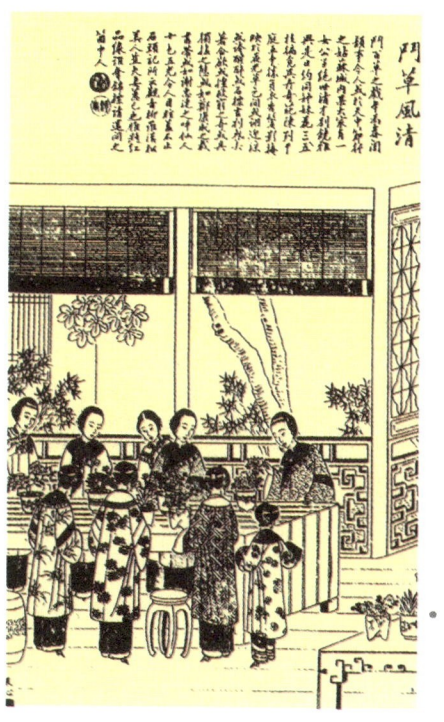

- 《斗草风清》（出自《点石斋画报》）

（图片提供：FOTOE）

Grass Stem Fight in the Breeze (from *Pictorial of Dianshi Zhai*)

生绵，黄昏疏雨湿秋千。"至明清时期，斗草之风依然十分盛行。

斗草主要有两种方式：第一种是文斗，即以每人采得的花草名作对，以种类多、品种奇为胜。文斗比拼的是文学素养，一般为文人雅士、女子等所喜爱。

第二种是武斗，即以每人采得的花草茎相互拉扯，比试草茎或叶柄的韧性，谁的草茎或叶柄后断就算谁赢。武斗强调的是单纯的竞技乐趣，一般为儿童所喜爱。

藏钩

藏钩，是一种猜度游戏，参赛者分为两组，其中一组将玉钩、银钩或其他小物件藏在一人手中，由另一组猜是藏于谁手中，猜中者胜出。

藏钩最早出现在汉代，源自汉武帝的宠妃钩弋夫人。汉代辛氏在《三秦记》中写道："昭帝母钩弋夫人，手拳而有国色，先帝宠之。世人藏钩法此也。"据传，钩弋夫人自打出生之后就一直紧握双手，且有美貌，被世人视为奇女子。汉武帝听说之后召她入宫，令其展开双手并赫然发现其

There are two kinds of grass stem fight: one is verbal fight. People write couplets with the names of the grass they have gathered, and the one who gathers the most kinds of herbs as well as the most exotic wins. With literary quality as the most important factor, this fight especially appeals to literati, celebrities and ladies.

The other one is a martial fight. Two contestants each pick a blade of grass that has some tenacity, then cross the blades and pull with strength. The one whose blade of grass stays unbroken in the end wins. Since this is purely about the fun of competition, it is especially popular among children.

Hook Hiding

Hook hiding is a game of guessing. Participants are divided into two groups, of which one hides a jade or silver hook or other small objects in someone's hand, and the other guess in whose hand it is hidden, and people who guess correctly will win.

This game firstly appeared in the Han Dynasty, and originated from a favored imperial concubine of Emperor Wu, Gouyi. As is recorded in *Story of Sanqin*

玉带钩（秦）
Jade Belt Hook(Qin Dynasty, 221 B.C.-206 B.C.)

手中攥有玉钩，于是便迎娶她入宫，号"拳夫人"。因其住在钩弋宫，故名"钩弋夫人"。此后，人们模仿钩弋夫人手中攥有玉钩而发明了藏钩游戏，并逐渐在宫廷和民间流传开来。

魏晋南北朝时期，藏钩已十分流行，并深受老人和儿童的喜爱。三国时期魏国文学家邯郸淳所著的《艺经》中有相关记载："腊日饮祭之后，叟妪儿童为藏钩之戏。"可见，藏钩是腊日（即农历十二月初八，俗称"腊八节"）祭饮之后，老人和儿童常玩的游戏。

唐宋时期，酒令盛行，藏钩就是其中一种。酒令是酒席上的一种助兴游戏。席间推举一人为令官，其他人听从令官的命令轮流说出诗词、成语等，违令者或说不出的人要罚酒。

by Mr. Xin in the Han Dynasty, "Imperial Concubine Gouyi is Emperor Zhao's mother. Born with two fists clenched, she is such a beauty and beloved woman of Emperor Wu. So people invented the hook hiding game to commemorate her." It is said that Imperial Concubine Gouyi was considered a legendary lady, who was born with two fists clenched as well as outstanding beauty. Hearing about this, Emperor Wu summoned her to courtyard and asked her to extend hands only to find that a jade hook was in her fist. Then she was granted Imperial Concubine Quan and also known as Imperial Concubine Gouyi because of living in Gouyi Palace. Henceforth, imitating Imperial Concubine Gouyi's anecdote, hook hiding was invented and was spread among royalties and common people.

During the Wei, Jin, Southern and

• 玉带钩（西汉）
Jade Belt Hook (Western Han Dynasty, 206 B.C.-25 A.D.)

• 青白玉嵌宝石带钩（明）
Greenish White Jade Hook Embedded with Gems (Ming Dynasty, 1368-1644)

藏钩游戏有"分为二曹，以交胜负"的规定，即分为两组，一组藏，一组猜，两组交替进行。藏的一组把钩握在本组一名成员的手中，猜的一组选出一个人来猜钩放在谁的手中，猜中则胜出。如果参与游戏的人数为奇数，多出的那个人则称作"飞鸟"，其可以自由选择加入哪一组。

Northern dynasties, this game had been very popular, especially among old men and children. In *Classic of Art* by Handan Chun, a writer of the Kingdom of Wei, it is recorded, "After drink offerings on Laba Rice Porridge Festival, elderly people and children all began to play hook hiding." It indicates that this game is frequently played by elderly people and children after drink offerings on Laba Rice Porridge Festival.

In the period of the Tang Dynasty and the Song Dynasty, games for entertainment when drinking prevailed, and hook hiding was one of them. It was played in this way: one person was elected to give orders and others were required to recite poems or idioms according to the orders. Those who violated the orders or failed to respond would be made to drink as a forfeit.

As is ruled by this game that participants are divided into two groups to compete, one group is required to hide the hook, the other to guess and the two groups switch roles after each set. Someone from the hiding group hides the hook in the hand of one of his group members, and then a person chosen from the guessing group will guess where the hook is hidden, and they will win if their

古代还有一种与藏钩类似的游戏，名为"射覆"。早在汉代时就已出现。相传，西汉的东方朔（前154—前93）是射覆的行家，有"射覆第一神人"的美誉，《汉书》中就有相关的记载。射即猜度，覆即覆盖，射覆是一种将东西覆盖起来，然后让另一个人进行猜度的游戏。射覆有原始射覆和文字射覆两种形式：原始射覆，就是用盆罐、大碗之类的东西去遮盖扇子、砚台

guessing is correct. If the participants are in odd numbers, the extra one is called "flying bird" and is free to join any group he wants.

Another game in ancient China similar to hook hiding is called *Shefu*. It has already appeared in the Han Dynasty. It is said that Dongfang Shuo of the Western Han Dynasty is an expert on *Shefu*, reputed as the No.1 player, which is also recorded in the *History of the Han Dynasty*. In ancient Chinese, *She*

• 钩弋夫人（图片提供：FOTOE）
Imperial Concubine Gouyi

等日常用品，让其他人猜。文字射覆，是在原始射覆基础上发展而来的，指猜度典故和句子后面所隐藏的文字。

means guessing and *Fu* means covering, therefore *Shefu* is a game in which one person covers up something and lets the other guess. There are two ways to play *Shefu*: firstly, original *Shefu*, in which people use things like basins, jars or big bowls to cover up daily supplies, such as a folding fan or an ink stone to let others guess; secondly, verbal *Shefu*, which evolved from original *Shefu*, and indicated letting participants guess the hidden characters behind the allusions or sentences.

- **东方朔像**

东方朔，西汉著名辞赋家，为人诙谐幽默且博学多识、言辞敏捷，著有《答客难》《非有先生论》等作品。

Statue of Dongfang Shuo

Dongfang Shuo, a famous poet of the Western Han Dynasty (206 B.C.-25 A.D.). He was not only humorous, but also knowledgeable and had a ready tongue. His representative works are *Da Kenan*, *About Mr. Feiyou*, and so on.

投壶

投壶，是古代传统酒令之一，是指将没有箭镞的箭矢投入壶中，以投入多者为胜，而输者则被罚酒的风雅游戏。

投壶源自西周时期的射礼，明代汪禔在《投壶仪节》中有相关记载："投壶，射礼之细也，燕而射，乐宾也。庭除之间，或不能弧矢之张也，故易之以投壶，是故投壶射类也。"由于人们在举行射礼时，常会受到场地、个人射箭水平等方面的限制，因此出现了更加简单易行的投壶礼。

"投壶"一词最早出现在春秋时期的史书《左传》中："晋侯以齐侯宴，中行穆子相，投壶。"讲述了晋国君主宴请齐国国君，在宴会上投壶礼以娱乐。"投壶"的壶即酒壶，广口大腹、颈部细长，壶中装有豆子，以防止箭矢投入后跃出。箭矢由棘木制成，不装箭镞和箭羽。

汉代时，投壶仍然有一定的等级限制，并延续以往的礼节规定：首先由司射主持仪式，击鼓奏乐，

Pitch-pot

As one of the traditional games in ancient China, pitch-pot is a kind of elegant game in which participants pitch arrows without arrowheads into a pot, and the one who pitches the most arrows into the pot wins and the loser will be punished by drinking.

Pitch-pot originates from archery of the Western Zhou Dynasty. In *Pitch-pot Etiquettes*, Wang Zhi of the Ming Dynasty recorded, "Pitch-pot is a variant of archery; archery was often practiced in the banquet to make fun, but sometimes it was not very convenient in the courtyard due to the limited space, therefore later on people began to play pitch-pot in replace of archery and we can conclude that pitch-pot is inspired by archery." The activity of archery was often affected by limited space, people's archery skills and other elements. Therefore, the pitch-pot which is simpler and more practicable comes into being.

As an entertainment activity among royalties, the Chinese words of "pitch-pot" first appeared in *The Commentary of Zuo*, a history book of the Spring and Autumn Period, as is written that the king of the State of Jin invited the king of State

● 投壶画像石（东汉） （图片提供：FOTOE）

画像中间位置立着一个酒壶，壶内有两支箭矢，旁边放着酒樽，内有一勺，宾主二人正抱矢投壶，形象地记录了汉代的投壶之礼。

Stone Relief of Pitch-pot (Eastern Han Dynasty, 25-220)

In the middle of the painting stands a wine put with two arrows inside it. Beside it, lies a wine goblet with a ladle in it. Both the host and the guest are holding arrows in hand to pitch into the pot. This picture vividly depicts pitch-pot etiquettes of the Han Dynasty (206 B.C.-220 A.D.).

主人和来宾就位；然后由主人为宾客递上箭矢，并相互施礼；待司射把壶放到宾、主面前，宣讲完规则后，比赛才正式开始。投壶受到士大夫、贵族的欢迎，每逢宴饮必以"雅歌投壶"助兴。东汉史书《东观汉记》中记载："取士皆用儒术，对酒娱乐，必雅歌投壶。"此时，壶中已不放豆子，箭矢改木制为竹制，投入后能够弹出，可以用来反复投掷。据史料记载，汉武帝时期有一个叫郭舍人的艺人，善于投壶，可以"一矢百余反"。

魏晋南北朝时期，出现了许多

of Qi to an official banquet, in which Zhonghang Muzi served as the master of ceremonies and pitch-pot was played for entertainment. In this game, it is a wine pot with wide mouth, big belly, long and thin neck that is used and there are also beans in the pot in case arrows bounce out later. The arrow is made of *Ji* wood without arrowhead and arrow feather.

When it came to the Han Dynasty, pitch-pot was still played according to hierarchy to some degree and stuck to old etiquettes as well: as the host of the ceremony, *Sishe* (official position, the one in charge of archery) would beat the drum and play music to welcome hosts

投壶专著，有《投壶变》一书传世。三国时期魏国人邯郸淳还作有《投壶赋》。这一时期，壶的形制有所改变，在壶口两旁增添了两耳，并增加了游戏的花样。例如，箭矢横在壶耳上称作"横耳"，箭竿斜倚在壶耳上称作"耳倚竿"，箭矢倒入壶中斜倚在壶耳上称作"侧耳"。

唐宋时期，投壶的礼仪性大大降低，成为民间、宫廷的日常娱乐活动。唐代诗人王建的《宫词》中写道："分朋闲坐赌樱桃，收却投

and guests in position; then the host gave arrows to the guests and they saluted each other; the game officially began after Sishe put the pot in front of the hosts and guests and preached game rules. Pitch-pot was popular among literati, officialdom and royalties. In banquets, people would have more fun by singing elegant songs and playing pitch-pot. *History of the Han Dynasty in Dongguan*, a history book of the Eastern Han Dynasty wrote that, "(in the Han Dynasty) The imperial civil service examination is all about Confucianism; people will sing elegant songs and play pitch-pot at the banquet

- 《朱瞻基行乐图卷》【局部】（明）
此幅描绘了明宣宗朱瞻基着便服在御花园中观赏各种游戏表演的场面，其中就包括投壶。
Painting of Zhu Zhanji's Recreations (Ming Dynasty, 1368-1644)[Part]
It depicts that Zhu Zhanji, Emperor Xuanzong of the Ming Dynasty in casual clothes is watching game shows in the imperial garden.

• 陶投壶（西汉）
Clay Pitch-pot (Western Han Dynasty, 206 B.C.-25 A.D.)

壶玉腕劳。"明清时期，投壶仍旧受到人们的喜爱。明宣宗朱瞻基、明武宗朱厚照都十分喜好投壶。清代时，社稷坛中设有投壶亭，以供祭奠活动后的娱乐游戏。

投壶比赛时，分成"主党"和"乡党"两组，主人站在左侧，客人站在右侧，每人手中各有四支箭矢，每投进一根，记一"算"（"算"即算筹，古代的一种计算木棒），放在

for entertainment." At that time, there were no beans in the pot and arrows were all made of bamboo rather than wood so that they could bounce out later and people could thus catch and repeat pitching. According to the historical records, Guo Sheren, an entertainer in the reign of Emperor Wu of the Han Dynasty was very good at this game. He could pitch an arrow into a pot, and when the arrow bounced out, he could catch and pitch it again, being able to repeat it about 100 times.

In the period of the Wei, Jin, Southern and Northern dynasties, there appeared many monographs on pitch-pot, of which *The Evolvement of Pitch-pot* has been handed down. Handan Chun of the Three Kingdoms Period (220-280) also wrote *Pitch-pot Poems*. During this period, the shape of pot changed a little bit by adding two ears near the two sides of the spout respectively and more rules were created for diversity. For example, the arrow perching on the pot's ear was called "horizontal ear"; the arrow reclining against the pot ear was called "leaning ear"; the arrow standing in the pot, leaning on the pot ear is called "side ear".

During the period of the Tang Dynasty and the Song Dynasty, pitch-

"中"（是一种鹿、马等形状的计分筒，上有八个小孔，可插入算筹）中。四矢投完为一局，采取三局两胜制，输者要罚酒。

pot became a daily entertainment activity than a kind of etiquette. Wang Jian of the Tang Dynasty wrote in *Palace Poem*, "Idle and lonely maids indulge in playing pitch-pot on a bet of cherries; they even feel a pain on their wrists because of tiredness." During the period of the Ming Dynasty and the Qing Dynasty, this game was still popular and Emperor Xuanzong, Zhu Zhanji, and Emperor Wuzong, Zhu Houzhao were also very fond of it. In the Qing Dynasty, a Pitch-pot Pavilion was built in the Altar of Land and Grain for entertaining activities after ceremonies.

In playing pitch-pot, the participants are divided into host party and guest party. The host party stands on the left and guests on the right. Each one holds four arrows. There will be one count (refers to a counting rod used to score), if an arrow is pitched into the pot. The counting rods are all put in *Zhong* (a scoring bucket in the shape of a deer or a horse with eight holes in which counting rods are inserted). Four rounds of pitching makes one set. The two out of three sets match is applied and the penalty for losers is drinking.

- 铜投壶（清）（图片提供：FOTOE）
此投壶是清代宫廷中的娱乐工具。
Copper Pitch-pot (Qing Dynasty, 1616-1911)

This pot is an entertainingt tool in the palace in the Qing Dynasty (1616-1911).

射礼

弓箭是人类在中石器时代发明的狩猎工具，之后逐渐成为武器。自商代起，射箭被视作男子必须掌握的基本技能，也是军事训练的重要组成部分。西周时期，射箭发展成为上层贵族阶级宴会上的重要礼仪，名为"射礼"。按照古代射礼规定，首先要挑选六名德才兼备的弟子来担任司射。两人为一组，称作"一耦"，共分三组，分别称为上耦、次耦、下耦。每一个射手都要发射四支箭。

Archery

Bow and arrow are hunting tools invented in the Mesolithic Age by human beings and later evolves into military weapons. Since the Shang Dynasty (1600 B.C.-1046 B.C.), archery has been considered as one of the indispensible skills for men and an important part of military training as well. During the Western Zhou Dynasty, archery became an important etiquette in the banquet among the upper class and therefore got its name. According to archery rules in ancient times, at first six men possessing both integrity and ability were elected as *Sishe* (official position in charge of archery). With two in each, they were divided into three *Ou* (means group), namely upper *Ou*, middle *Ou* and lower *Ou*. Each shooter would launch four arrows.

> 益智类游戏

九连环

九连环，又称"智环""巧环"，是传统益智玩具，一般由九个以环杆串联的圆环及一个长形框柄组成，有金属、玉石、竹木等多种材质。解九连环就是将九个圆环与长形框柄依次分离，先解开者为胜。

战国时期的哲学家庄子所著的《庄子·天下篇》中的"连环可解也"，被认为是目前为止关于拆解连环的最早文字记载。元代杂剧家郑光祖撰有杂剧《丑齐后无盐破连环》，讲述的是战国时期，秦国、燕国欲联兵攻齐国，先派使者给齐国送玉连环，故意进行刁难。齐宣王的皇后钟无艳虽奇丑无比，

> Puzzle Games

Chinese Ring Puzzle

The Chinese ring puzzle, also called intelligent ring or talent ring, is a traditional puzzle game, composed of nine rings connected rods and a rectangular frame. Most of them are made from metal, jade, bamboo and wood. To solve the ring puzzle need to disconnect all the nine rings from the rectangular frame. The fastest one wins the game.

The famous philosopher Zhuangzi in the Warring States Period once stated in his book *Zhuangzi, Chapter of the Country*: the ring puzzle can be solved. It is considered as the earliest document referring to the Chinese ring puzzle. The drama writer Zheng Guangzu in the Yuan Dynasty wrote *Ugly Queen of State Qi Solving the Ring Puzzle*, telling the story that: in the Warring States Period, State

• 吴友如《妙绪环生》（清）

此图描述了四个上海妇女和一个小男孩在解九连环的情景。

Solving Ring Puzzle, by Wu Youru (Qing Dynasty, 1616-1911)

It depicts a scene in which four Shanghai women and a little boy try to solve the Chinese ring puzzle.

却有勇有谋。她不但顺利解开了玉连环，还率兵打败了秦、燕两国。《战国策》中也有关于解玉连环的记载，可见战国时期，人们已经将解连环视作一种益智游戏。

相传西汉才女卓文君作有一首《怨郎诗》："一别之后，二地相悬；只说是三四月，又谁知五六年；七弦琴无心弹，八行书不可

Qin and State Yan intended to attack State Qi together. So they sent an envoy to State Qi and delivered a jade ring puzzle to stir some troubles. The Queen of King Xuan of State Qi was very ugly yet extremely intelligent. She not only solved the jade ring puzzle but also defeated the joint army of State Qin and State Yan. Also, there are several records about the jade ring puzzle in the book *Strategies of the Warring States*, which indicates that the game of Chinese ring puzzle prevailed as a puzzle game in the Warring States Period.

In the Western Han Dynasty (206 B.C.-25 A.D.), the talented lady Zhuo Wenjun wrote a poem *Blaming for Lover*, "After farewell, we separated, thought it was three or four months, now it has been five or six years, do not have the mood to play the seven-stringed lyre, eight lines of letter can not express my yearning, nine-ring puzzle was broken, ten miles pavilion I am waiting for you, hundreds of thoughts and thousands of lovesickness, I can do nothing but blame it for you, my lover." Each line starts with a figure and mentioned the nine-ring puzzle.

In the Song Dynasty and the Yuan Dynasty, the Chinese ring puzzle was prevalent, not only among the nobles

传；九曲连环从中折断，十里长亭望眼欲穿。百思想，千系念，万般无奈把君怨。"每一句诗都是以数字开头，其中就提到了连环。

宋元时期，解连环游戏已十分流行，不仅是贵族们的游戏，在民间也广为流传。北宋词人周邦彦的词作《解连环·怨怀无托》中就有关于解连环的描述："纵妙手、能解连环，似风散雨收，雾轻云薄。"明清时期，解连环更是被列入"京都四百十四行"。明代杨慎在《升庵集》中写道："今按连环之制，玉人之巧者为之。两环互相贯为一，得其关捩解之为二，又合而为一。今有此器，谓之九连环，以铜或铁为之，以代玉。闺妇儿童以为玩具。"明代时，九连环改玉制为铜制、铁制，是当时妇女和儿童的玩具。清代时，一位署名"贮香主人"的作者编写了一部名为《小慧集》的百科全书，其中记载了九连环的详细解法，并配有插图。

九连环和七巧板、华容道被称为"中国三大古典智力游戏"，民间素有"拆不开的九连环"之说，

but also the common people. There are several lines about solving the ring puzzle in the verse *Solving Ring Puzzle, Resentment*, written by Zhou Bangyan: with talent, the ring puzzle can be solved as breeze blowing away the rain, like light fog and thin cloud.

In the Ming Dynasty and the Qing Dynasty, the Chinese ring puzzle was listed among the Four Hundred and Fourteen Professions in Beijing. Yang Shen in the Ming Dynasty once wrote in his book *General Record of Sheng An*: according to the formal structure, the talented jade artisan produced a jade ring puzzle that two strung rings can be disconnected with a trick. Nowadays, it is called the Chinese ring puzzle, made from copper or iron to replace the precious jade material. It serves as toy for women and children. In the Qing Dynasty, a writer named Master Zhuxiang compiled an encyclopedia *Collection of Tips and Tricks*, which includes the solving instruction of Chinese ring puzzle and also the relevant illustrations.

The Chinese ring puzzle and tangram and Huarong Path Escape are considered as the Three Classical Puzzle Games in China. And the saying of the unsolvable Chinese ring puzzle is also heard among

框柄：有剑形、如意形、蝴蝶形、梅花形等多种形状，以所有连环从其上取下为胜。
Frame handle: It is in sword shape, *Ruyi* shape, butterfly shape, plum blossom shape, etc. The one disconnecting all the rings from the frame handle wins the game.

连环：圆形，由环杆一一相连。
Connecting rings: They are in circle, being connected with rods.

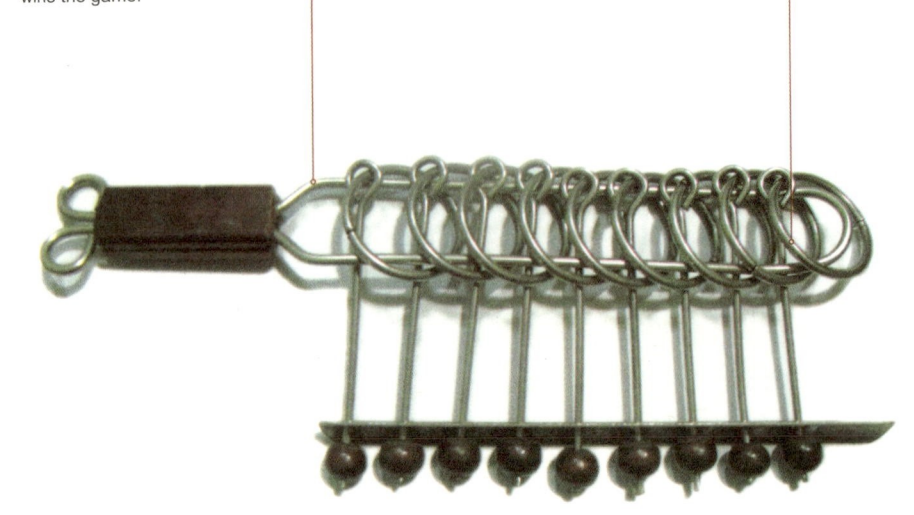

• 九连环
除了九连环之外，还有鱼环、蝶环、蜻蜓环、凤凰环、锁环、壶环、钟环、塔环等多种连环玩具。
Chinese Puzzle
Aside from Chinese puzzle, there are fish ring, butterfly ring, dragonfly ring, phoenix ring, lock ring, pot ring, bell ring, pagoda ring and other relevant ring puzzle toys.

可见解九连环是一项需要技巧和耐心的游戏。玩家需要将九个连环上下移动，一共进行341次才能解开九连环。九连环的每个环互相制约，只有第一环能够自由上下。要想解下或套上某个环，就必须满足两个

the folks, which indicates the Chinese ring puzzle requires technique and patience. The player should move the nine rings in a particular pattern for totally 341 times to solve the game. The nine rings of the puzzle are linked with each other. Only the first one can be

条件：第一，前面的一个环在框柄上；第二，除了前面一个环之外的环全都不在框柄上。掌握了这一规律才能成功解开九连环。九环除了可以从框柄上全部解下，还可以摆出宫灯、绣球等多种形状。

七巧板

七巧板，又称"益智图""智慧板""唐图"，由五块大小不一的等腰直角三角形、一块正方形和一块平行四边形的木板组成，故名。这七块木板拼合在一起是一个正方形。

七巧板大约源于唐代宫廷宴会

- **七巧板**（图片提供：微图）
Tangram

moved. In order to disconnect or connect a particular ring, two conditions should be satisfied: first, the previous ring is on the frame handle; second, except the previous ring, other rings are not on the frame handle. Only by mastering this law can the game be solved. Aside from being disconnected from the frame handle, the Chinese ring puzzle can be displayed in different shapes like lantern, strip ball, etc.

Tangram

The tangram, also called talented puzzle, intelligent puzzle, Tang's puzzle, etc., is composed of five wooden pieces of isosceles right triangle with different sizes, a piece of square and a piece of rhomboid, hence the name. The seven pieces can make up a bigger square.

The tangram probably originated from the table-and-bench puzzle played in the banquet in the courtyard of the Tang Dynasty, which was called *Yanji* (燕，*Yan*) or *Yanji* (宴，*Yan*, meaning banquet). It was a indoor game to place the tables and benches into different shapes, like T-shape or 山-shape (*Shan*, meaning mountain) to force the guests to constantly change their seats and

• 七巧桌进酒图案
Tangram Tables

上的拼儿游戏，即燕几，又称"宴几"。这是一种将几张不同形制的桌几拼合成"T"字形、山字形等，使得宾客不断变换座位、方位，以增添宴会欢乐气氛的室内游戏。

宋代文学家黄长睿改进了燕几，在原有基础上又增加了一个正方形的桌子，使其拼合的图案更富有变化，因此燕几又名"七星桌"。黄长睿为此编撰了《燕几图》一书，共收录了76种拼合形

directions so as to activate the ambience in the banquet.

In the Song Dynasty, the scholar Huang Changrui made some improvements on *Yanji*. He added a square table to the original set to get richer possible variants. So the *Yanji* got another name Seven-star Table. And Huang also compiled the book *Collections of Yanji*, which includes 76 final shapes composed by the tables. He stated, "*Yanji*, with endless

状。他在书中写道："燕几图者，纵横离合，变态无穷，率视夫宾朋多寡，杯盘丰约，以为广狭之则。"

明代文人戈汕在前代燕几的基础上设计了蝶几，因桌子拼合起来形似蝴蝶，故名。在操作原理和用途上，蝶几与燕几基本一致，只是在桌子的数量和形制上有了很大的改进：从原有的七个桌子增加到十三个，并依据勾股三角形的理论增加了三角形的桌子，可以拼合成

combinations, mostly fits for the entertainment in the banquet regardless of the number of the guests."

In the Ming Dynasty, the scholar Ge Shan designed a butterfly puzzle (the final result is in the shape of butterfly, hence the name), called *Dieji*, based on the formal *Yanji*. In terms of operating principle and function, the butterfly puzzle was similar to the *Yanji*, except for the number of tables and shapes. It needed 13 tables instead of 7. Moreover, it added a triangular table according to the Gougu Theorem (Pythagorean Theorem). So the butterfly puzzle could display more than one hundred shapes, which was more delicate than *Yanji*. Ge Shan also wrote a book *Collections of Dieji* to record all the display shapes.

In the early Qing Dynasty, the large and heavy *Dieji* gradually evolved into tangram which was more delicate and convenient. At once, the tangram earned appreciation from the noble and the common people. In 1813, the book

• 鸟形图案
Bird-shaped Tangram

一百多种不同的形状，比燕儿更加巧妙。戈汕将蝶儿拼合图案汇编成《蝶儿谱》一书。

清代初期，体积大而笨重的蝶儿逐渐演变成为更加小巧、易于操作的七巧板，受到贵族和普通民众的喜爱。1813年，碧梧居士编著、桑下客绘制的《七巧图合璧》一书出版，这是中国现存最早的七巧板专著。现存最早的一块七巧板是由美国商人罗伯特·沃恩于1802年从广州购得的，为象牙材质。1805年，欧洲出版了一本名为《中国儿童新七巧图》的专著。可见，七巧板已经逐渐在世界范围流传开来。

七巧板可以拼合成三角形、正方形等几何图形，以及人物、动物、桥梁、房屋等多种趣味图形，数量达上千种，对于开发智力十分有益，是中国常见的儿童益智游戏。

华容道

华容道是一种滑块游戏，与魔方、孔明棋（即独立钻石棋）一起并称为"智力游戏界的三个不可思议"。

Collections of Tangram, written by Biwu Jushi and drawn by Sangxia Ke was published. So far, it is the earliest treatise of tangram in China. And the oldest existing tangram was bought from Guangzhou City in 1802 by an American businessman Robert Vaughan, which is made from ivory. In 1805, there was another book about tangram *New Collections of Tangram in China* was published in Europe. Obviously, the tangram prevailed across the world at that time.

The tangram can make up more than one thousand shapes, including triangular shape, square shape and other geometric shapes, as well as figures, animals, bridges, houses and other interesting abstract shapes. It is good for exploring intelligence. So it has become one of the most common puzzle games in China.

Huarong Path Escape

Huarong Path Escape is a kind of block sliding game, and is called Three Incredible Puzzle Games together with magic cube and Kongming chess (solitaire).

Huarong Path Escape was inspired by the historical story about Cao Cao's

赵云 Zhao Yun　　曹操 Cao Cao　　黄忠 Huang Zhong　　马超 Ma Chao　　卒 Pawn

关羽 Guan Yu

张飞 Zhang Fei

- **华容道"横刀立马"阵法**（图片提供：俄图）

此阵法是最常见的华容道阵法，共需81步才能将被九个棋子围困的"曹操"移出。

Tactical Deployment of Holding the Knife on the Horse in Huarong Path Escape

It is the most common deployment in Huarong Path Escape, which requires 81 moves to move Cao Cao to the exit.

华容道游戏源自《三国演义》中曹操败走华容道的历史故事，是民间流行的一种益智游戏。华容道由十个棋子和一个棋盘组成，棋

escape from Huarong Path quoted in *The Romance of the Three Kingdoms*. It is a popular puzzle game among the folks. It is composed of one chessboard representing the Huarong Path and ten

子大小不一，分别代表曹操、关羽、张飞、赵云、黄忠、马超和四个小卒。棋盘则代表华容道，下方边框有出口。走华容道，就是通过移动除"曹操"外的其他九个棋子的位置，摆出不同的阵法，包括"横刀立马""近在咫尺""过五关""水泄不通""小燕出巢"等共计几十种，帮助"曹操"通过棋盘最下方的出口移出棋盘。

所有的棋子摆放进棋盘后，棋盘中会有两个空着的小方格，要通过这两个空着的小方格不断移动棋子。其过程中不允许跨越棋子或者叠放棋子，直到"曹操"逃出为止。游戏中，只有"曹操"能离开棋盘，以移动次数最少者为胜。

chess pieces of different size respectively representing Cao Cao, Guan Yu, Zhang Fei, Zhao Yun, Huang Zhong, Ma Chao and four pawns. At the bottom of the board, there is an exit. Playing the Huarong Path Escape is to move the other nine pieces (except for Cao Cao) to present tens of different tactical deployments including holding the knife on the horse, near at hand, defeating five pawns, tightly packed, swallow leaving the nest, etc. to help Cao Cao move through the bottom exit.

After placing all the pieces in the board, there will be two little square slots left empty via which the pieces can be moved. It is not allowed to step over the other pieces or overlap with others. The player should keep moving other nine pieces to make a clear path for Cao Cao to escape. In the game, only Cao Cao can leave the board. And the one who completes the game with the least moves wins the game.

麻将

　　麻将是一种四人牌类益智游戏，基本打法简单，容易上手，且玩法多样，故深受普通民众的喜爱。

　　关于麻将起源的说法不一，一般认为起源于江苏太仓的护粮牌。明代时，江苏太仓曾建有皇家粮仓，储存着大量的稻谷。当时，雀患频发，损失了大量粮食，只能靠人工捕捉麻雀的方式来减少损失。

Mahjong

Mahjong is a card puzzle game played by four persons. The rules are simple and the playing methods are various. So it is widely appreciated by the common people.

There are different versions about the origin of mahjong. Generally, it is believed the mahjong originated from the barn card invented in Taicang City, Jiangsu Province. In the Ming Dynasty, there are imperial barns built in Taicang City which stored tons of rice and grain.

- 麻将
  Mahjong

管理粮仓的官吏为了奖励护粮的士兵，发明了一种竹制筹牌，用来记录捕捉麻雀的数目，并以此牌为凭证发放赏金，即"护粮牌"。因为筹牌上刻有数字和符号，因此逐渐演变成了一种游戏。在太仓方言中，"麻雀"和"麻将"读音相近，此牌便得名"麻将"，又称"麻雀牌"。

当时的麻将有三种基础牌式，分别名为"万""索""筒"，点数从一至九。"万"用汉字"万"来代表，是指赏钱的单位，表示赏钱的数量。"索"用麻雀图案来代表，是指用细绳串起来的麻雀，表示捕捉麻雀的数量。"筒"用圆圈来代表，是指枪筒，几筒就代表几支火枪。此外，还有"东、西、南、北"风和"中""白""发"等牌式。风是指风向，在用枪打麻雀时需考虑风向，有东、西、南和北四个风向。"中"指射中，涂红色，又称"红中"。"白"用白板来表示，指放空枪没有射中。"发"即发放赏金，有发财之意。除了牌式之外，打麻将时的术语也与捕雀护粮有着密切关系。例如，

At that time, the sparrow infestation occurred a lot, which cost a large amount of rice and grain. The local could only diminish the loss by catching the sparrows manually. Hence, in order to reward the guards of the barns, the local official invented a bamboo chip card to record the number of the captured sparrows and granted the reward to the owner according to the chip card. So it was also called Barn Card. As the card was carved with numbers and symbols, it gradually evolved into a game. In the dialect of Taicang, the pronunciation of sparrow is similar to the one of mahjong. So this game was called mahjong or sparrow card.

There were three basic card patterns, namely *Wan*, *Suo* and *Tong*, respectively numbered from one to nine. *Wan* was represented by the character *Wan* (万), indicating the unit of reward and the number indicates the amount of the reward. *Suo* was represented by the picture of sparrow strung by the rope indicating the number of the captured sparrows. *Tong* was represented by circles indicating gun barrels or the guns. Besides, there were patterns of eastern, western, southern and northern winds and " 中 " (*Zhong*), blank (*Bai*) and 发 (*Fa*).

People Playing Mahjong (Minguo Period, 1912-1949)

The wind (including eastern, western, southern and northern winds) indicated the wind directions which should be taken into account while shooting the sparrows. *Zhong* indicated the effective shot, painted in red color, also called red *Zhong*. The blank was represented by blank tile, indicating the missed shot. *Fa* indicated to giving out the reward and gaining fortune. Aside from the patterns, the jargon of mahjong is also related to the sparrow capture. For example, *Peng*, indicated the gunshot and a fallen sparrow. It was a *Peng* when others discarded a certain tile which could make a set of three same pattern tiles together with the two same pattern tiles in the player's hand. *Hu*, indicated the eagle sent by the guards to capture the sparrow, meaning win the game.

In the Qing Dynasty, the mahjong prevailed from the courtyard to the common lanes. Nowadays, it becomes a common game in people's daily life. In Sichuan Province, people are even more enthusiastic about mahjong.

"碰"即"嘭"，代表枪声响起，麻雀被打死，玩法是当其他人出了某张牌之后，如果自身手里有两张与之相同的牌，便可获得该牌。"和（hú）"即鹘，指放出鹘鹰后可以成功捕捉麻雀，意即得胜。

清代时，无论在宫廷还是民间打麻将都十分流行。如今，打麻将已经成为人们日常生活中常见的游戏项目，在四川地区更是有"全城一片麻，家家二五八"的说法。

麻将主要由竹子、骨头或塑料等材料制成。最为常见的麻将样式为136张牌，基本牌式包括"饼""条""万"三种，点数从一至九，每个点数有四张牌，即有三十六张"饼"，三十六张"条"，三十六张"万"，以及"东""西""南""北""中""发""白"各四张。打麻将时，首先要掷骰子来决定庄家，之后由庄家开始抓牌，游戏才正式开始。

The mahjong is mainly made of bamboo, bone or plastic material. The most common set has 136 tiles with the basic patterns of *Bing* (circle, cake), *Tiao* (rope, chain) and *Wan*, respectively numbered from one to nine. Each number has four tiles, so there are 36 tiles of *Bing*, 36 tiles of *Tiao* and 36 tiles of *Wan*, as well as four tiles of East, West, South, North, *Zhong*, *Fa* and blank respectively. While playing, the banker should be determined by dice throw. And then the players start to take the tiles and the game begins.

• 四川民众在茶馆打麻将（图片提供：FOTOE）
Sichuan People Playing Mahjong in Tea House

> 休闲类游戏

抖空竹

抖空竹，又称"抖空钟""扯铃"，是一种抖动绳子使空竹在空中旋转不坠落的休闲游戏。

明代时，空竹就已经出现，名为"空钟"，玩法与现在略有不同，《帝京景物略》中详细记载了空钟的玩法。空钟由竹木制作而成，中空，形似倒立的铜钟，故名。人们用绳子和带孔的竹尺分别向左右方向用力勒住其上方的木柄，空钟就会急速旋转。空钟的旁侧开有哨口，旋转时可发出响声，十分动听。

清代时，抖空竹在民间已十分常见，清代的《燕京杂记》中详细记载了京都燕京（即北京）

> Casual Games

Playing *Kongzhu* (Diabolo)

Playing *Kongzhu* (diabolo), also called playing *Kongzhong* or pulling bell, is a casual game in which the player should keep pulling the rope to drive the *Kongzhu* rolling in the air.

In the Ming Dynasty, the *Kongzhu*, named *Kongzhong* at that time, has appeared. The playing pattern was different from the present ones. In the *Record of the Life in Beijing*, it refers the information in detail. *Kongzhong* (*Zhong* meaning bell) was made from bamboo, with hollowed belly and upside-down bell-shaped appearance, hence the name. Players rein the upper wooden handle with rope and holed bamboo ruler and pull them to the opposite directions with strength to drive the *Kongzhong* spinning swiftly. There is a whistle at the side

● 放空钟图
在明定陵出土的红素罗绣平金龙百子花卉方领女夹衣的背面有一幅《放空钟图》。

Putting Kongzhong
It is a design on the back of a red silk lined dress with square-cut collar and embroidered with golden loongs, which was excavated from the Dingling Mausoleum of the Ming Dynasty.

儿童抖空竹的场景："京师儿童有抖空竹之戏，截竹为二短筒，中作小干，连而不断，实其两头，窍其中间，以绳绕其小干，引两端而撇抖之，声如洪钟，甚为可听。"抖空竹逐渐由民间传入宫中，成为宫中嫔妃们的休闲游戏。如今，每年的春节庙会上都会有卖空竹的摊位，抖空竹成为人们日常健身、杂耍的重要活动。

空竹由圆盘和木轴组成，圆盘上开有哨口。按照组成部分的不同，空竹可分为单轮、双轮、双轴、双轮多层和异型等多种形式，其中以单轮和双轮最为常见。单轮空竹由一个圆盘和一根木轴组成，双轮空竹则是由两个圆盘和一根木

of the *Kongzhong* to make sound while rolling.

In the Qing Dynasty, *Kongzhu* became more and more common in the street. In the book *Jotting of Beijing*, written in the Qing Dynasty, it refers the scene of children's playing diabolo in ancient Beijing (Yanjing), "The children living in Yanjing often play diabolo which is made from bamboo tube. The diabolo has a hollowed belly and solid two ends. While playing, the player should wrap the rope around the belly and keep pulling two ends to drive the diabolo spinning and making sound." Gradually, the diabolo was introduced to the imperial palace and became a casual game enjoyed by the imperial concubines. Nowadays, in the temple fair on the Spring Festival, there are stalls selling diabolo and it has already become one of the common activities and leisure games in China.

- 单轮空竹（图片提供：微图）
Single-wheeled Diabolo

- 双轮空竹（图片提供：微图）
Double-wheeled Diabolo

轴组成，抖动时更容易掌握平衡。

抖空竹的基本方法是：人们将两端带有木杆的线绳缠绕在空竹木轴上，拎起之后双手来回扯动，使空竹在空中持续旋转。此外，抖空竹还有"金鸡上架""翻山越岭""鲤鱼摆尾"等花样玩法。例如，"金鸡上架"就是将空竹快速旋转之后，解开缠绕在木轴上的线绳将空竹抛向空中，然后用抖杆接住，使之在棒上转滚或转到另一根抖杆上。"翻山越岭"就是将空竹

The diabolo is made up by round plate with whistle opening and wooden beam. According to different structures, the diabolo can be divided into single-wheel, double-wheel, double-beam, double-wheel with multiple layers, alien type etc. The most common types are the single-wheeled and double-wheel. The singe-wheeled diabolo is made up by a round plate and a wooden beam; the double-wheeled diabolo is made up by two round plates and a wooden beam, which is more convenient to keep the balance.

The basic instructions are: the

北京街头卖空竹的摊位（民国）(图片提供：FOTOE)
Diabolo Stalls on Beijing's Streets (Minguo Period, 1912-1949)

抛向空中后用线绳接住或再抛起。"鲤鱼摆尾"是用脚踩住线绳中部，使在脚一侧转动的空竹由脚背上跃过至另一侧，来回交替。

抽陀螺

抽陀螺，又称"打老牛""抽冰尜"。陀螺多为木制圆锥形，上粗下尖，放于地上用绳鞭用力抽动后可直立旋转。

陀螺被认为是中国最古老的玩

player should wrap the rope (with two stick handles at two ends) around the diabolo's wooden beam and lift it in the air and pull the rope back and forth to keep the diabolo spinning in the air. Besides, there are various techniques like Golden Rooster on the Shelf, Climbing Mountains, Carp Swaying Its Tail, etc. For example, the Golden Rooster on the Shelf indicates the technique of unwrapping the rope on the wooden beam and throwing the diabolo into the sky and then catching it with the stick handles to keep it spinning on the stick or between the two sticks; Climbing Mountains indicates the technique to throw the diabolo in the sky and catch it with the rope and over and over again; Carp Swaying Its Tail indicates the technique to fix the middle part of the rope with one foot to force the spinning diabolo jump over the instep over and over again.

Spinning Top

The spinning top, also called whipping old ox or whipping ice top, is generally a wooden cone with a tapering bottom tip,

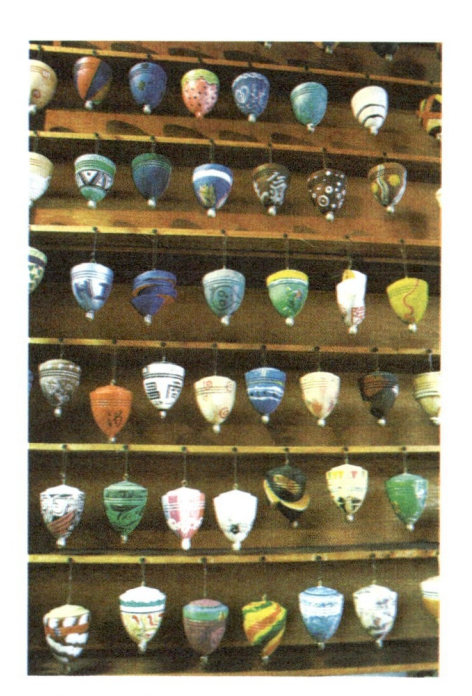

多彩的木陀螺（图片提供：FOTOE）
Colorful Wooden Spinning Tops

具之一，至少有四五千年的历史，且材质多样。陕西西安半坡遗址、山西龙山文化遗址都曾出土过陶制陀螺，江苏常州马家浜文化遗址曾出土木陀螺，距今5000年左右的山西夏县新石器时代遗址还曾出土过石陀螺。

关于陀螺的最早文字记载出现在北魏时期，农学家贾思勰在《齐民要术》中写道："梜者，旋作

which can keep spinning on the ground while being whipped with rope.

With at least four or five thousand years' history and diversified materials, the spinning top is considered as one of the oldest toys in China. There were several clay spinning tops unearthed from Banpo Remain in Xi'an City, Shaanxi Province and Longshan Culture Remain in Shanxi Province. Wooden spinning tops were once excavated from the Majiabang Culture Remain in Changzhou City, Jiangsu Province and stone spinning tops were found in the Remains of the Neolithic Age. In Xiaxian County, Shanxi Province.

The earliest written record about spinning top appeared in the Northern Wei Dynasty (386-534). A famous agronomist Jia Sixie states in *Qimin Yaoshu*, "Jiayu (a type of wood) can be used to produce spinning top (*Duyue*) and wine cups." *Duyue*, indicating the spinning top, is a toy for children. In the book *The Past of Wulin* written by Zhou Mi in the Southern Song Dynasty, the terms *Qianqianche* and wheel disc indicate the spinning top. In the capital city of the Southern Song Dynasty, Lin'an (today's Hangzhou City), there were many toy stores selling kite, shuttlecock

独乐及盏。"梜榆木可以用来制作独乐和杯盏。独乐即陀螺，是儿童的玩具。南宋词人周密在其笔记《武林旧事》中记载的"千千车轮盘"，也是指陀螺。当时的首都临安城（今浙江杭州）中有许多经营各种玩具的小商店，店内出售的商品包括风筝、毽子和陀螺等。

"陀螺"一词最早出现在明代，《帝京景物略》中记载了当时的一首民间童谣："杨柳青，放风筝；杨柳活，抽陀螺；杨柳

● 陀螺与绳鞭 （图片提供：微图）
Spinning Tops and Whips

and spinning top.

The term spinning top first appeared in the Ming Dynasty. According to *Record of the Life in Beijing*, there was a ballad, "While willows turning green, fly the kite; while willow blooming, play the spinning top; while willow turning yellow, play the shuttlecock." It is clear that the spinning top prevailed among the folks at that time. Meanwhile, it was introduced into the palace and became the leisure game for maids. At that time, the spinning top was rolled directly by hands, called *Zhuangyu*. First, a border should be drawn and the spinning top can not cross the border. After a while of spinning, if the top appears to be slowing down or leaning aside, the player is allowed to whip the top with sleeve. The one who keeps the top spinning for the longest time wins the game. Later, the move of whipping with sleeve gradually evolved into whipping with rope.

Nowadays, there are various kinds of spinning top, including paper spinning top, bamboo top, wooden top, thread beam top, copper thread top, plastic top, etc., with different size. Due to its convenience and simple instruction, the spinning top has become an important casual game in people's daily life.

- 抽冰尜（图片提供：微图）

抽冰尜是中国东北地区对抽陀螺的称呼，冬季一般在冰上进行。光滑的冰面可以使陀螺的旋转更加顺畅，同时也增添了乐趣。

Spinning *Bingai* (Ice Top)

Spinning ice top (*Bingga*) is the special term for spinning top in the Northeast China Region, which is generally performed on the ice in winter. The smooth ice surface can speed up the spinning and add more fun.

黄，踢毽忙。"可见，当时在民间抽陀螺已十分流行。同时，陀螺还传入宫廷，成为宫女们打发时间的游戏。当时，陀螺的玩法是用手直接旋转，称作"妆域"：首先要划定一个区域，陀螺旋转时不能出界。陀螺旋转一段时间后出现停转或歪倒迹象时，允许用衣袖拂拭，以旋转时间长短判断输赢。后

Cricket Fighting

Cricket fighting, is also called *Ququ* fighting, *Cuzhi* fighting or *Qiuchong* fighting. The cricket is famous for its beautiful chirping. In the *Notes on Kaiyuan and Tianbao Periods*, it records that, "In the autumn, the women in the imperial palace would feed crickets in golden cages and place them beside their pillow to enjoy the chirping. And the

来，袖拂的动作逐渐演变成了绳鞭抽打的形式。

如今，陀螺的类型十分丰富，有纸陀螺、竹陀螺、木陀螺、线轴陀螺、铜线陀螺、塑料陀螺等，形制大小不一。抽陀螺以其简单、方便的特点，成为人们日常休闲娱乐的重要活动。

斗蟋蟀

斗蟋蟀，又称"斗蛐蛐""斗促织""斗秋虫"。蟋蟀以鸣叫悦耳闻名。《开元天宝遗事》中记载："每至秋时，宫中妃妾辈，皆以小金笼捉蟋蟀，闭于笼中，置之枕函畔，夜听其声。庶民之家皆效之也。"该记载反映出了唐代时妃嫔、宫女将蟋蟀饲养在笼中，以及此俗扩散至民间的情形。人们在饲养蟋蟀时发现，雄性蟋蟀常因抢夺食物、领地或配偶而相互撕咬，于是便利用雄性蟋蟀好斗的习性，观其互斗以娱乐。

南宋时期，斗蟋蟀的风气最为盛行，无论是皇室贵族还是普通百姓都以斗蟋蟀为乐。宋理宗时，丞相贾似道十分喜爱斗蟋蟀，故将其

common people also liked to imitate such activities." It reflects the prevalence of the cricket feeding in the Tang Dynasty. Soon, people found that the male cricket often picked fights with others due to food, territory or couple. So making use of cricket's aggressive habit, people started to enjoy watching cricket fighting.

In the Southern Song Dynasty, the cricket fighting prevailed across the country and was attractive to the nobles and common people. In the reign of Emperor Lizong, the Prime Minister Jia Sidao was obsessed to the cricket fighting, so he changed the name of his mansion in Geling Town, along the West Lake in Hangzhou City into Fighting Hall. Jia was proficient in cricket fighting and feeding. He wrote the first book about insects in the world, named *Classic of Cuzhi*, which introduced the knowledge on the catching, buying, feeding, fighting, curing, and breeding of the cricket. However, he was scolded for the disordered governing capability. There was a well-known saying that there is no Prime Minister in the courtyard, yet a cricket fighting expert along the West Lake.

In the Ming Dynasty and the Qing Dynasty, the cricket fighting reached its full bloom. In the *Record of Chang'an*

位于今杭州西湖葛岭的住处命名为"斗闲堂"。贾似道对于斗、养蟋蟀十分精通，撰写了《促织经》一书。书中详细介绍了关于蟋蟀的捕捉、收买、喂养、斗胜、医伤、治病、繁殖等方面的内容。但因其不理政事、昏庸无能，当时民间流传着"朝中无宰相，湖上有平章"的说法。

明清时期，斗蟋蟀之风达到鼎盛。明代文人蒋一葵撰写的《长安客话》中记载了当时京师人们斗蟋蟀的盛况："瓦盆泥罐，遍市井皆是，不论老幼男女，皆引斗以

written by Jiang Yikui in the Ming Dynasty, it depicts the grand occasion of cricket fighting in Beijing, "Clay basins and pots are everywhere along the streets. Regardless the age or gender, everybody enjoys the fun of cricket fighting." In the Qing Dynasty, in the autumn, people will take the cricket fighting as the major entertainment. Someone even built a special arena for cricket fighting. In the *Qing Jia Lu* written by Gu Lu, it states, "Around the White Dew (in September), feeding cricket and cricket fighting broadly prevailed across the country, which was called *Qiuxing*."

- **青花云龙纹蟋蟀罐（明）**

  民间有"玩虫一秋，玩罐一世"的俗语。蟋蟀罐是斗、养蟋蟀的必备工具，同时也是精美的收藏品。

  Blue-and-white Porcelain Cricket Pot with Cloud and Loong Pattern (Ming Dynasty, 1368-1644)

  Among the folks, there is a saying that feeding the cricket for one season and collecting the cricket pot for one life. The cricket pot is the common equipment for cricket fighting, as well as an exquisite collection.

• 苏汉臣《秋庭婴戏图》【局部】（北宋）
Children's Playing Cricket Fighting in Autumn Yard, by Su Hanchen (Northern Song Dynasty, 960-1127)[Part]

为乐。"清代时，每年秋季，无论是市井儿童还是达官贵族都以斗蟋蟀来娱乐。有人还设置了专门的场所，以供人们赌斗蟋蟀。清代顾禄撰写的《清嘉录》中曾有相关记载："白露前后，驯养蟋蟀，以为赌斗之乐，谓之秋兴。"

斗蟋蟀时，将两只大小相差不多的蟋蟀放置在中间设有隔板的罐中，然后双方主人先用特制的马尾鬃挑弄蟋蟀。例如，触碰其头部、尾部，蟋蟀会作出敏捷的反应；触

In the game, participants will put their own crickets (with similar size and figure) into the pot separated by a clapboard. Then they will try to provoke the crickets with specially processed horsetail, like touching its head or tail to make the cricket perform swiftly and touching its cercus or rear legs to make it turn around. Then taking away the clapboard, the two crickets meet and the game begins. After being provoked, the crickets become more aggressive like combative soldiers. Once the two crickets touch each other, they will start to chirp

碰其尾须、后腿，蟋蟀会立即掉转头。然后将隔板去掉，两只蟋蟀相遇后，游戏就正式开始了。经过挑弄的蟋蟀斗性增强，像意气风发的士兵，双方一旦相碰，就会一边发出鸣叫一边相互撕咬，直到其中一方被咬死或逃走才算结束。人们一般称善斗的蟋蟀为"将军"。

按照颜色的不同，蟋蟀的等级也有所不同，一般以青色的蟋蟀为最优，白色的蟋蟀为最差。《帝京景物略》中记载："以青为上，黄次之，赤次之，黑又次之，白为下。"蟋蟀生长的地方对其品质也有很大影响。《促织经》中记载："出于草土者，其身则软；生于砖

and bite each other until one of them dies or escapes. People often called the most aggressive cricket General.

According to the color, the level of the cricket varied. Generally, the indigo cricket is the best and the white one is the worst. In the *Summary of Sceneries in the Capital City*, it records, "The indigo is the top; the yellow is the second; the red is the third; the black is the fourth and the white is the lowest." The growing environment of the cricket also closely relates to its quality. In the *Classic of Cuzhi*, it explains, "The one born in the grass soil is soft; the one born in the brick is tough; the one born in the grassland, barren land, bricks, deep pits or the land exposed to the sun is stubborn." The fighting cricket should have a round head and big teeth, with round legs and long cirrus, a broad neck and a tough figure, as well as a loud chirp.

Hide-and-seek

Hide-and-seek, also called *Cangmao'er*, touching elephant, blind touching, is a casual game participated by two or more players. As a favorite game among children since ancient times, hide-and-seek is very popular, which brings a lot

• 紫砂蟋蟀罐（清）
Cricket Pot Made from Purple Clay (Qing Dynasty, 1616-1911)

• 吴友如《蟋蟀会》（清）
The Party of the Cricket Fighting (Qing Dynasty, 1616-1911)

石者，其体则刚；生于浅草瘠土砖石深坑向阳之地者，其性必劣。"斗蟋蟀一般以头圆牙大、腿圆须长、项宽毛燥、形身阔厚、叫声明亮者为最佳。

捉迷藏

捉迷藏，又称"藏猫儿""摸象""摸盲盲"等，是一种两人或多人的躲藏游戏。作为古今儿童喜爱的游戏，捉迷藏在儿童间十分流

of fun to people's childhood.

The written record about hide-and-seek can trace back to the Tang Dynasty. The poet Yuan Zhen once wrote in his poem *Memory*, "In the cold night I wandering along the corridor, can not tell the strange fragrance in flower clusters. Only remember in the dim moonlight, we played hide-and-seek in childhood." This poem depicts the scene that he and his lover played hide-and-seek in moonlight. So it can be told that this game was

行，为他们的童年生活带来欢乐。

关于捉迷藏的文字记载最早见于唐代，唐代诗人元稹（779—831）在《杂忆》一诗中写道："寒轻夜浅绕回廊，不辨花丛暗辨香。忆得双文胧月下，小楼前后捉迷藏。"此诗描述了作者与恋人在月下小楼前捉迷藏的情景，可见当时捉迷藏是在夜间进行的。宋代时，捉迷藏也是夜间玩耍的游戏。花蕊夫人在《宫词》中写道："内人深夜学迷藏，遍绕花丛水岸旁。乘兴或来仙洞里，大家寻觅一时忙。"

performed at night in times. In the Song Dynasty, this game was still played at night. In the *Palace Verse* written by Lady Huarui, "We played hide-and-seek at night, running across the flower shrubs to the river bank, even hide in the mountain cave, others just can not find her."

The hide-and-seek has three steps, namely closing eyes, hiding and finding. First, the catcher's eyes should be covered with a handkerchief and others should find a place to hide as soon as possible; after a limited time, the catcher

• 吴友如《儿童捉迷藏》（清）
（图片提供：FOTOE）
Hide-and-seek, by Wu Youru
(Qing Dynasty, 1616-1911)

捉迷藏 (图片提供：FOTOE)
Hide-and-seek

捉迷藏分为迷、藏、捉三个步骤。首先要用手绢蒙住捉人者的眼睛，其他人则各自寻找地方躲藏。在规定时间后，捉人者开始寻找躲藏起来的人，这时躲藏起来的人不能再移动位置。在中国各地捉迷藏的名称有所不同，但玩法大抵相同。陕西称之为"盲人摸象"。所有人围成一个圈，站在圈中央的一个人用手帕蒙住双眼，被称作"盲人"。游戏开始后，"盲人"要去摸周围的人，被摸到的人不能出

can search for other players. Then the hidden players can not move anymore. In China, the name of the hide-and-seek varies from place to place. However, the playing rules are the same. In Shaanxi Province, it is called "the blind touching elephant": all the players stand in a circle and the one standing in the center should cover his/her eyes to be the "blind". When the game begins, the "blind" should try to find others and speak out the name of the person he/she touches. Other players can not make a sound. The one that gets caught and identified should be the "blind" next round.

Raree Show

The raree show, also called picture show, or western scene, originated from the Tongzhi Period (1862-1874) of the Qing Dynasty, which prevailed in Beijing and Shanghai. In 1930s, two famous street artists named Big Golden Teeth and Little Golden Teeth performed

声，直到盲人准确判断出是谁才算胜出，而被猜中的人则要充当"盲人"。

拉洋片

拉洋片，又称"拉大片""西洋镜"或"西洋景"，起源于清代同治年间，在北京、上海等城市十分流行。20世纪30年代的北京天桥上，有艺名为大金牙、小金牙的师徒二人，他们就是以拉洋片为生的街头艺人。清代末年，在春节庙会上观赏拉洋片成为普通群众重要的娱乐活动。

raree show for living in Tianqiao. In the late Qing Dynasty, the raree show had become an important activity in temple fair for the public.

The raree show is usually performed by one person, with the major equipment including a scenery case (a double-layer wooden case) and simple musical instruments like gong, drum and small cymbals. In the performance, the artist will pull the rope outside the scenery case to drive the pictures in the case moving while playing musical instruments and singing songs to explain the story of the pictures. The viewer can watch the moving pictures in the case through the magnifying lens installed on the case. The pictures are generally about natural landscapes, figures and historical stories.

Raree show includes several types, namely West Lake scenery, water case, big foreign ship, etc.

The West Lake scenery mainly presents the scenery pictures of the West Lake, including Dawn on the

- 《北京民间风俗百图·拉洋片》（清）
  One Hundred Pictures About Folk Customs in Beijing—Raree Show (Qing Dynasty, 1616-1911)

拉洋片的表演者一般只有一人，工具主要包括一个景箱（木箱，一般为双层）和锣、鼓、镲等简单的乐器。演出时，艺人拉动景箱外的绳子，景箱内的画片就会随之转动，同时艺人还会敲打乐器并配以唱词来解释画片上的内容。观者通过景箱上安装的放大镜来观赏转动的画片。画片多以风景、人物

Su Causeway in Spring, Three Pools Mirroring The Moon, Fish Viewing at the Flower Pond and Melting Snow at Broken Bridge, hence the name. There are four magnifying lenses on the scenery case. The artist pulls the rope outside the case to move the eight pictures inside the case.

The water case shows a series of pictures and a puppet embedded in the last one by pulling the rope and

- 一群青年人在看拉洋片（图片提供：微图）

景箱分上、下两层，上层有展示画和"西洋镜"字样等，下层则是镶有凸透镜的暗箱，内有画片。

A Crowd of Young People Watching Raree Show

The scenery case has two layers, the upper and the bottom. The upper layer presents the pictures and the Chinese characters for raree show, and the bottom layer is embedded with the hidden box of convex lens in which there are pictures.

和历史故事等内容为主。

拉洋片有西湖景、水箱子、大洋船等多种样式。

西湖景。因画片多为杭州西湖景色，如苏堤春晓、三潭印月、花港观鱼、断桥残雪等，故名。景箱上嵌有四块放大镜。表演者拉动景箱外面的绳索，箱内的八张画片在箱内上下移动。

水箱子。表演者拉动绳索，景箱内的画片随之上下移动，最后一张画片上镶有立体的偶人，可以随着表演者的拉动而做出各种动作。景箱底部放有水槽，可通过小水管取水灌入水箱形成细流，与人偶的舞动相映成趣。水箱子的画片内容大都与水有关，如《水漫金山》等。

大洋船。因景箱形似轮船，故名。与水箱子一样，大洋船内也装有偶人。拉动景箱外的绳索，偶人就会舞动。

turning the pictures. The puppet can present various movements according to the story. There is a water channel at the bottom which can be filled with water through a small water pipe to form a dynamic effect responding to the movement of the puppet. The story mainly relates to the water, like the chapter of *Flooding the Jinshan Temple*.

The big foreign ship has a ship-shaped appearance, hence the name. Similar to the water case, it also has a puppet that can move while the artist pulls the rope outside the case.